NORTH POLE
99705
ALASKA

SANTA CLAUS
47579
INDIANA

NOEL
64854
MISSOURI

MISTLETOE
41351
KENTUCKY

*Christmas greetings to everyone everywhere!*

HOLIDAY
34690
FLORIDA

RUDOLPH
54475
WISCONSIN

ANTLERS
74523
OKLAHOMA

SNOWFLAKE
85937
ARIZONA

PARTRIDGE
40862
KENTUCKY

GARLAND
75043
TEXAS

# An Old-Fashioned Christmas

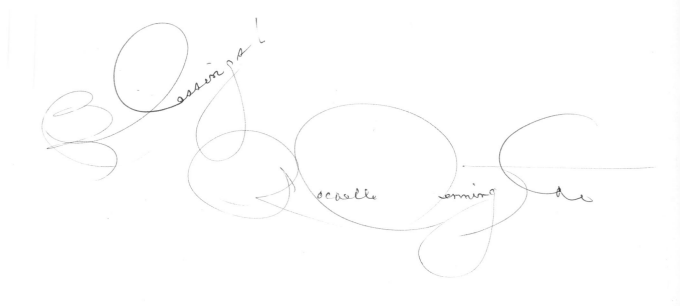

All images included in this book were used by permission of the copyright holders with appreciation from the authors:

Mr. Potato Head image: *Mr. Potato Head, registered trademark, copyright 2008 Hasbro, Inc.; used with permission.*

Barbie doll image: *Barbie appears courtesy of Mattel, Inc. Copyright 2008 Mattel, Inc. All rights reserved.*

Schwinn bicycle image: *Courtesy of Pacific Cycle, Inc., Madison, Wisconsin.*

Copyrights continued on Acknowledgments page at rear.

The authors wish to extend heartfelt gratitude to Sarah Vollmer-Griffin, Graphic Design Specialist at EP•Direct, as well as to her entire staff, for their tireless dedication to this project. (WTHR)

Grateful acknowledgment is made to Linda Vis, Rochelle's dear friend, for her expert research assistance.

Rochelle wishes to thank her husband, Leslie, for all of his love and support over the past thirty years. He is at the heart of everything she accomplishes.

Printed in Canada

**Pathways Press**
**1-800-503-5507**
**www.AnOldFashionedChristmasBook.com**

**ISBN: 978-0-9740810-4-5**

# An Old-Fashioned Christmas

**Tinsel, Gingerbread Men & Billie-the-Brownie**

*Rochelle Pennington and Nicholas Pennington*

**Published by Pathways Press**

**1-800-503-5507**

# Table of Contents

*Dedicated to Great Grandma Serwe*
*who still believes in Santa Claus*

Cathy Stern

# Let it Snow!

Heap on the wood!
The wind is chill!
But let it whistle as it will!
We'll keep our Christmas merry still!

SIR WALTER SCOTT

# Let it Snow!

Do you remember snow? Not the fluffy few inches today's weathermen call a "blizzard," but the thick blankets from days past when drifts crept halfway up the sides of homes and buildings. Shoveling out your car didn't mean scooping snow from around it, but it could, at times, literally mean un-burying the hidden vehicle. Driving over snowy roads could also be a challenge—especially if snowbanks were higher than your car.

Weather forecasting, too, has changed from the bygone days of earlier decades when all you needed to predict a coming storm was a current issue of *The Old Farmer's Almanac,* or to listen to elders who insisted they could predict a snowstorm because they could "feel it coming in their bones." Much of forecasting in earlier years was done "by guess and by golly."

With the arrival of November, and sometimes as early as late-October, you knew winter would soon be wrapping itself around the land, dusting it sparkling white. Southbound geese faded from view, and fetching the morning newspaper was accompanied by the sight of your own

**1936 Gas prices**

**"To grandmother's house we go!"**
SNOWY ROADS, 1936

frosted breath, floating in front of you, the white puffs of smoke suspended in mid-air.

Children impatiently anticipated the first snowfall of the season while writing letters addressed to Santa Claus with wishes for ice skates and sleds—along with "Can you please make it snow?" requests. For many folks, a snowy landscape meant Christmas was coming as surely as the first sight of a candy cane.

Familiar holiday carols emphasized the chilliness of the season with lyrics like "let it snow," "walking in a winter wonderland," and "I'm dreaming of a white Christmas."

When the long-awaited flakes started falling, usually long before Christmas—or the two-week vacation from school that followed it— youngsters ran to the window, and then outside. Winter's arrival brought with it the sound of boots stamping on the front porch and the sight of soggy mittens drying on the woodstove or radiator. Blankets and quilts were pulled closer at nighttime as blustery winds crept in through the cracks of houses. Single-paned windows kept the snow out, but allowed the cold to penetrate in. And each new morning brought with it a unique icy painting, drawn from the brush of old Jack Frost himself.

Mothers and fathers reminded youngsters to shut outside doors more quickly. "We're not heating the outside!" they scolded. "Were you raised in a barn?!" Thrift was a way of living, whether it concerned food or fuel. After all, money didn't "grow on trees."

Many homes were kept warm with firewood heaped high outside

A chilly chore

> "Winter brings delights unmatched by other seasons—a frozen pond, a snow-covered field, sparkling icicles dangling from the eaves, the crunch of boots on the snow."
>
> **JESSICA KERRIGAN**

on wood piles. Hard-working fathers, with broad shoulders and calloused hands, tended woodstoves and fireplaces, and kept their axes sharp. Smoke rose from chimneys, curling into the forever sky, beckoning those outside to quicken their step and come sit by the fire. A cup of mulled cider, flavored with Christmasy spices, was always a welcomed treat while unthawing by the fireside in December if you had a nipped nose or were numb with cold.

Old Man Winter woke up "on the wrong side of the bed" many mornings as the days grew shorter and colder. Fast-falling snow could create whiteouts when the season closed in, greatly reducing visibility and halting travel—even local travel. This would, predictably, cause an excitement among entire populations of neighborhood children as they realized school would undoubtedly be cancelled, freeing up a full day for playing in the snow.

Parents unpacked winter wardrobes from cedar closets—woolen

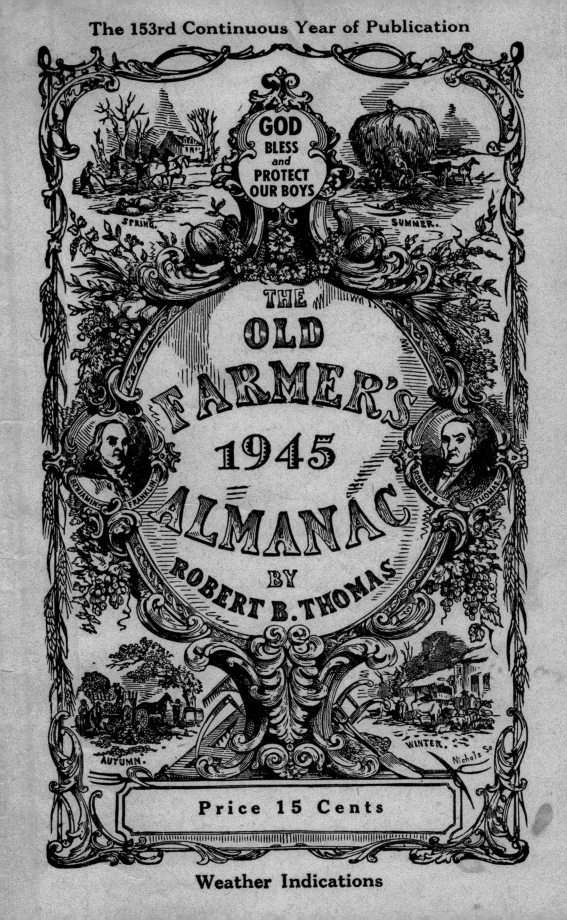

GOD BLESS and PROTECT OUR BOYS

SPRING.

SUMMER.

THE OLD FARMER'S 1945 ALMANAC BY ROBERT B. THOMAS

AUTUMN.

WINTER.

Nichols Sc

Price 15 Cents

Weather Indications

sweaters, turtlenecks, flannel shirts, knee-socks, ear muffs, and thermal long underwear. ("Long johns" were widely worn by both genders to combat brisk temperatures.) Boys and girls layered warm garments as protection against the chill of winter before heading outside into the splendor of a whitened world. Even snowmen remembered to bundle up; they were often seen wearing hats perched on top of their very round heads and mittens tucked over the ends of their branched arms. A big bowl of Cream of Wheat cereal, served warm, or Quaker oatmeal, sprinkled with cinnamon and sugar, helped keep bellies toasty, fortifying youngsters against the cold before they headed out into the snow.

Playful boys and girls poured from house doors, filling their lungs with fresh air, catching nickel-sized snowflakes on their tongues as they ran to backyard sheds. They rushed through creaking garage doors and into dusty corners where ice skates, in many sizes, hung with knotted laces looped from rusty nails. Seasonal toys were pulled from atop rafters. Little hands clutched short ropes attached to sleds and wooden toboggans, stretching many feet long, as the winter vehicles were towed to "the hill," the highest and steepest slope in town. Metal sleigh runners left an unmistakable trail as they were dragged across trackless, freshly-fallen snow.

Toboggans, lengthy enough to carry a half-dozen of your closest cousins, lined the crests of favorite sledding spots. Vertical views from these hilltops could be quite dramatic—especially if they were known by dangerous-sounding nicknames like "Dead Man's Drop" or "Point of No

**Christmas morning, 1938**

Return"—adding to the sense of adventure. Excited riders, sometimes as many as eight, would scrunch forward, making room for yet one more. Whisking off and picking up speed, riders would hang on to one another tightly, "for dear life," letting out screams—"wheeeeeeeeeeeeeee"—that would begin at the top of the hill and persist to the bottom. The whole charade would end in a tangled mess of limbs and laughter. Then, it was back up the hill, with huffing and puffing, and heart rates doubling, for more merriment.

Whether a runway was a straight shot down, or a curvy path with twists and turns, warmly-clad youngsters filled many wintry afternoons going up the hill, and down the hill, up and down, all afternoon long until it was time to drag their aching legs home. The fun would resume another day when mothers urged, "Go outside and play!"

High-pitched voices also begged fathers to shovel driveways and walkways when snow arrived in measurable accumulation so elaborate forts and "igloos" could be crafted, between which a barrage of snowballs would later fly.

When you're a ten-year-old boy, nothing feels quite so good as a freshly-packed snowball in the palm of your hand, squeezed and pressed into formation between your gloved, yet numb, fingers; except, perhaps, spotting a few of your friends within launching range. Neighborhood boys battled in friendly competition to see who had the better aim. (Worse than being pegged with a speedy snowball, however, was the infamous surprise of being ambushed by a friend with a handful of snow, quickly stuffed down the back of a shirt, or more dreadful, a pair of pants.)

Youngsters spent hours digging intricate systems of tunnels when the snow fell many inches deep, burrowing into high-piled snowbanks lining driveways, attempting to construct the largest fort in the neighborhood.

The outskirts of plowed parking lots also produced another snowy playground for frosty entertainment. Tall piles lining the edges, the tallest in town, would be deemed suitable for a spontaneous game of "king of the mountain." Screams and laughter would fill the air as smaller-bodied members of the group were sent tumbling down the slopes and, almost as quickly, went scrambling back up again in valiant attempts to take dominion of the higher territory. Others, preferring only to watch the roughhousing, lay in the snow on their backs, spread-eagled, with frozen smiles and noses rather red, creating snow-angels in all shapes and sizes.

Shaking the powdery snow from their shoulders, youngsters would then combine their efforts rolling growing balls of snow, in hopes of constructing the biggest snowman ever. Driving through town, entire families of snowmen could sometimes be spotted.

Lakes and swiftly-flowing rivers offered another favorite winter pastime when the waters froze solid—ice skating. Shovels were gathered and hometown "ice rinks" were swept clean of snow, readying the ice for wintry fun. Sharpened skates were laced snugly around ankles, and skaters, with rose-blushed cheeks, swirled and twirled, pretending to be world-class Olympians. The sound of metal blades carving figure-eights into the fresh ice echoed through riverbed arenas and across lakes. Some of the more

"Let's meet!  Let's go sledding!"

"When?"

"Tomorrow!  Day after tomorrow!  Next week!"

"We'll dig a snow cave!  We'll sled all night!"

"If there's a wet snow, let's all come back to school!  Let's start a big snowball!  Let's roll it down the hill until it's as big as the schoolhouse!"

"Yeah, and maybe knock the schoolhouse down!"

From *The Land Remembers*
by Ben Logan

A friendly snowman was "topped off" with a tractor tire and
a 50-gallon metal drum in 1955.

> ## Did you know . . .
>
> **The world's tallest snowman, according to the *Guinness World Book of Records*, was erected in Maine. The colossal giant measured 113 feet high (*11 stories!*) and used nine million pounds of snow!**

daring and adventurous skaters could, on a windy day, use bed sheets for sails, each skater holding an edge of an outstretched sheet, catching the breeze, and "sailing" down an icy stretch, gliding along the glassy surface.

Boys and girls, with noses dripping, then traced their footsteps home. Everyone traded smiles as the memory-making day came to a close. Years later, these grown-up youngsters would recall happy hours from their vanished youth, remembering a time when money was scarce, but fun was plentiful. And they'd long to return.

# *All I Want for Christmas*

"Christmas was lights and colors, warmth and laughter, and remembered voices. It was the feel of heavy brown wrapping paper, the tune of a music box, the smell of an orange, and the feel of a finely-worked turtleneck sweater that no older brother had ever worn."

BEN LOGAN

# All I Want for Christmas

Who remembers the popular Christmas song of the 1940s and 1950s, *All I Want for Christmas is my Two Front Teeth?*

Two front teeth. Some kids were so easy to please, weren't they? Most, however, hoped for a bit more than filling the gap in the middle of their grin when the holiday neared. Christmas meant Santa Claus was coming—with a bulging sack of toys, full to the brim—and *that* was surely a reason to smile!

Dreams whirled through the imaginations of youngsters—visions of "sugar plums," red wagons, bouncy balls, and yo-yos. And Raggedy Ann dolls, tinkertoys, roller skates, and puzzles. And jack-in-the-boxes. And Lincoln Logs and erector sets. And, of course, "a pony."

Boys imagined the excitement of racing through their neighborhood, downhill and through back alleys, on a shiny, new scooter. They could almost feel the grip of rubber on the handlebar as they kicked off in their mind, rolling faster and faster!

They could hear the "vrooooooooom, vrooooooooom" of matchbox cars driving across their mother's hardwood kitchen floor through grooved-lane "roads" in the wooden planks. And they could see themselves wearing the

Mr. and Mrs. POTATO HEAD
the joyful toy of 1001 faces!

new cowboy suit Santa would surely bring—a suit complete with hat and boots, badge and chaps, and a pistol in the holster. *Oh, the thrill of being sheriff of the entire household, upholding the law of the West while shouting "giddy up" and "yee haw" from the top of a playroom rocking horse, swinging a length of rope to lasso the family dog!* Nearly every 10-year-old boy wanted to be just like Davy Crockett. Or Hopalong Cassidy riding his horse, Topper. Or Roy Rogers riding Trigger. Surely, there were more cowboys wearing fringed, leather vests and firing cap guns in American backyards between 1930 and 1960 than you could have found on the entire frontier of the 1800s. "Howdy, partner!" was as familiar a greeting between elementary school boys as "Hey! Do you want to play?"

Pig-tailed girls could sense their maternal instincts as they thought about caring for a china dolly with a delicate, painted face and blinking eyes staring upward, lifelike. Visions of cradles and baby buggies danced through their heads. And tea sets, too.

They imagined what song would chime from the opened lid of a hand-wound jewelry box, a tiny ballerina figurine twirling circles within, or what words Chatty Cathy would speak when they pulled on her string. Would they be "please brush my hair" or "tell me a story"?

Some kiddies even sent Santa the catalog and page number for each item on their list. *So helpful!* Boys and girls thumbed through thick "wish books" which were delivered to family mailboxes by Sears and Roebuck, Montgomery Ward, and J.C. Penney. Others made sure to include specific instructions for what *not* to bring—especially socks and underwear. They were fearful that valuable space in their stocking would be used for items they would surely receive from Grandma or Aunt Mabel.

---

**"Even a man is a child when Christmas comes."**

**LANSING CHRISTMAN**

---

**Lionel Trains** make a Boy feel like a Man and a Man feel like a Boy

Letters to the North Pole, with misspelled words and all, would often address more than the subject of gift giving. Some letters were inquisitive: *Do you stuff pillows in your tummy? Why don't you ever change your clothes? Will you please find my daddy a job like yours so he only has to work one day a year? Who brought you presents when you were a kid? Are you friends with the Easter Bunny? When you asked me if I was good, did you mean* that day, or, like *all year?*

Other letters tried to confess less-than-perfect behavior in barely-readable scrawl: *I tried to be good, but I have five older brothers.* Young boys wrestled with the temptation to be naughty before the ink on their letter to Santa had time to dry.

Some letters included bribes: *I'll leave you a bottle of my daddy's whiskey if you bring me what I want.*

Letters included concern for Santa's health, as well: *I am not giving you any cookies because you are too fat already.*

Santa. Christmas wouldn't be the same without him, would it? Nor would it be the same without the humorous and heartwarming letters delivered to him annually with wishes for everything from baseball bats that "only hit homeruns" to new siblings: *Dear Santa, Last year I asked you for a baby brother; this year I want you to take him back.*

TO: SANta          FROM: TOmmy
    NOrtH PoLE
WiLL yOu giVE mE a nEW
tRaiN fOR CHRiStmas cuZ my
daddy KEEps pLaying WitH tHE
OnE yOu bROt mE LaSt yEar.

THIS pitcHer WaS dRawn by mE.

Santa's unique character possessed, and still does, the ability to simultaneously create in a child's mind the emotions of apprehension and overwhelming joy. Santa represents authority—and yet he represents friendship and familiarity at the same time. He is magical, and yet real enough to touch—at least once a year. And this encounter usually happened at the local department store in days past. (The first commercial Santa appeared in Philadelphia in 1841.)

It was one thing to hear about Santa and the North Pole, with its gigantic candy cane rising upward from snowy banks, marking the location of the fabled kingdom, but it was quite another when jolly old St. Nick showed up in person—*right in front of your eyes!* The sight of Santa Claus sitting squarely in front of you—waiting to ask "What would you like for Christmas this year?"—filled some boys and girls with unbridled excitement, and others with anxiousness and unease, especially toddlers and waddlers who were visibly nervous about making the acquaintance of the white-bearded, red-suited Mr. Claus for the first time.

Many of the presents requested at these annual chats were decided upon on the very day children walked through the crowded aisles of the

> **"I stopped believing in Santa Claus when I was six-years-old. My mother took me to see him in a department store and he asked me for my autograph."**
>
> **SHIRLEY TEMPLE**

**Barbie Millicent Roberts**
**Born: March 9, 1959**
**Hometown: Willows, Wisconsin**

store's toy department with their parents on their way to see Kris Kringle, or as they passed decorated windows filled with elaborate displays. Wonder was awakened in the eyes of boys and girls who stood on tippy-toes as they watched locomotive train engines, puffing real smoke, chug past windows and into tunnels, re-emerging further down. *What a thrill!*

It was a time when merchandise lining store shelves was American-made, constructed with craftsmanship and care by hardworking fathers who carried metal lunch boxes to factories down the street. It was a time when there was pride in doing a job well—"an honest day's work for an honest day's pay." Quality—it meant something. So did the words "Made in the U.S.A."

Tinkertoys were manufactured

in Evanston, Illinois, and Red Ranger cowboy outfits came from Wyandotte, Michigan. Erector sets were manufactured by the A. C. Gilbert Company in New Haven, Connecticut, and Lincoln Logs were produced in Chicago by Frank Lloyd Wright's son, John, who invented them. If you purchased a puzzle with interlocking pieces it probably came from the Built Rite Toy Company in Lafayette, Indiana, or from the Warren Paper Products Company located in the same city.

Santa Claus left presents under a tree decorated with tinsel from the National Tinsel Manufacturing Company in Manitowoc, Wisconsin, and with Shiney Brite ornaments produced in Hoboken, New Jersey.

> Deer Mr. Claus,
> I reely, reely, reely want a snake, a monkee, and a tiger. I already have a dog, a kittee, a goldfish, a birdee, a hamster, a turtle, a bunnee, and a frog. Pleez!
> Your friend, Billie
> P.S. My mother does not know about this letter.

Santa. His visitation on Christmas Eve was marked by cookie crumbs and missing milk. And it all started with a visit to his lap!

Wee ones lined up in front of Santa's throne, waiting expectantly as they inched forward where they would whisper, in a faintly audible voice, their secret wish for a paper doll or a puppet into the waiting ear of the one who had the power to grant it. One by one, children were invited, beckoned for a personal meeting to discuss this very important matter of present requests. Santa wanted to hear about each hoped-for toy firsthand. Children were careful not to ask for too much (but not too little either), in fear that Santa might think them selfish and put their name on the "naughty" list.

There could be other moments of mischief in the lively scene as youngsters who had visited Santa repeatedly in the past—especially boys— became curious enough, and brave enough, to sneak a quick tug at his beard to test its authenticity. *Ahh, the opposing forces of naughty and nice were always at work!* And Santa Claus was very interested in finding out which of these two had gotten the best of each child during the preceding year.

No, visiting Mr. Claus was not all fun and games! There was always this small matter of business that needed to be covered first—the annual behavior check. Lads and lasses collected their thoughts, waiting for the inevitable—and all-important—question: "Have you been a good boy or girl?" An uncomfortable pause, and a bit of squirming, usually followed. Very few youngsters approached Santa with the assured posture of being quite certain that their name had been pre-recorded on the "nice" list.

# Toys Likely to Appear Under the Christmas Tree

## 1930 - 1960

1931:   Dick and Jane books  ("See Dick run!  Go, Dick, go!")

1934:   Shirley Temple doll, Betsy Wetsy doll (dampened her diapers)

1935:   Monopoly (bestselling board game in the world)

1939:   Viewmaster, Red Ryder air rifle

1943:   Chutes and Ladders

1945:   Slinky

1947:   Tonka toys

1948:   Scrabble

1949:   Candy Land, Silly Putty, Cooties  ("I've got cooties!")

1950:   Radio Flyer Coaster Wagon

1951:   Colorforms

1952:   Matchbox cars, Mr. Potato Head

1956:   Play-Doh, Yahtzee, Uncle Milton's Ant Farm

1957:   Frisbee

1958:   Legos, Hula Hoop, Skateboard

1959:   Chatty Cathy doll, Barbie doll

1960:   Etch A Sketch

The question was a tricky one because there was no fooling Santa. After all, "he sees you when you're sleeping, and he knows when you're awake," right? But how good was good enough?

There was often a noticeable change in behavior prior to visiting Santa, notably an increase in a child's willingness to do chores, in hopes of gaining a spot on the "nice" list. This extra effort always seemed to work. It proved to be just enough to grant relief and happiness to every boy and girl returning from the lap with smiles on their face. "See, Mom!" they announced. "I *was* good!"

Yes, Santa's shiny, black boots would be coming down the chimney yet again, and little ones were left wondering how he managed to fit his rotund body down the narrow shaft year after year, and back up again, without so much as a grunt to wake the slumbering family. Santa *must* be magic for he was the size—and shape—of, well, his sack full of toys! He existed in a child's mind as surely as they did. Children believed in Santa and the North Pole, while their parents knew he lived more certainly in hearts and minds. Yes, Santa was real—even if he only existed in the form of someone who loved you dearly.

---

**"My first copies of *Treasure Island* and *Huckleberry Finn* still have some blue-spruce pine needles scattered within their pages. They smell of Christmas still."**

**CHARLTON HESTON**

---

As Christmas neared, boys and girls also thought on the gifts they would *give*, not just receive. They made sure Mom and Dad would have something special to open on the gladdest day of the year, too. These were special presents, as they usually had more to do with the creative use of craft

*Did you know . . .*

Howdy Doody was a television celebrity from 1947 until 1960. (Only 20,000 Americans owned television sets in 1947.)

The original puppet used in 1947 to launch the program was temporarily named Elmer, and the show was originally called "Puppet Playhouse." ("Howdy doody" was a greeting the puppet used.)

"The Howdy Doody Show" was the first television program to be broadcast in color, and the first network show to air five days a week.

Howdy ran for President in 1948. He placed third, receiving more votes than the political Progressive Party candidate, Henry Wallace. Howdy's campaign promises included:
All banana splits will have four scoops of ice cream.
Admission to rodeos and circuses will be free.
History books will include more pictures.
Christmas will be celebrated three times a year.

Howdy Doody lit the Rockefeller Center Christmas tree in 1953. Youngsters requested Howdy Doody toys for Christmas including books, stickers, board games, belt buckles, lunch boxes, and puzzles.

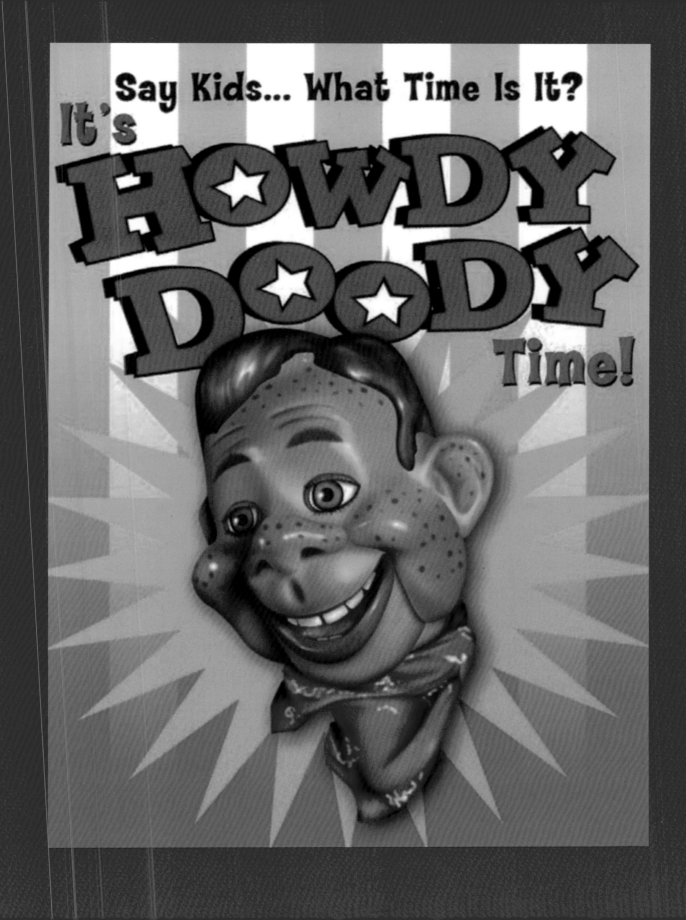

supplies than they did with saving a week's worth of allowance money. Finger-painted handprints and handwritten poems on construction paper decorated kitchen walls after the holidays, along with hand-drawn crayon pictures and paint-by-number artwork. Presents made in school were smuggled home, hidden in book-bags, undetected, and stowed secretly beneath beds to lie in wait for Christmas morning when they would be taken out of hiding, the creator proudly exclaiming, "I made this myself!"

Other presents were sometimes made possible by a healthy collection of pennies, safely stored in a piggy bank all year long. These wee "life-savings" were then carried in change purses to the local five-and-dime store, like F. W. Woolworth or Ben Franklin, where a new hankie for mother might be chosen or a small bottle of Old Spice aftershave for Daddy.

Many old-fashioned Christmases were not as well-funded as those of today, especially during the lean years of the Great Depression, but they were no less merry, to be sure. Fathers would find a way to provide—even through another jobless year. Bread lines stretched for blocks, and soup kitchens helped to put a little warm nourishment in cold bellies. Men stood in long lines for food, and in longer lines for employment, when the depression was at its worst. Families learned from necessity how to make a few meager dollars stretch to afford a simple holiday.

Parents "made do" during these years of prolonged economic downturn when there was little more to give than their love, and offered their sons and daughters as exciting a Christmas morning as possible with inexpensive toys and homemade gifts. Fathers' weathered hands carved toy-chests from scraps of lumber. Doll-houses were painstakingly constructed with tools on a basement workbench. Lamp-lit windows told of parents crafting homemade gifts late into the long hours of the night after their children were bedded down, sound asleep.

Mothers kept busy during this period of time, too, with their own handiwork. A new dolly for Christmas, quite possibly, could have been an impossible wish to grant, but there still could be a new dress for the old dolly. Or a stuffed teddy bear with button eyes, stitched by hand from leftover fabric. Every house had a sewing machine and a mother who knew how to use it. Pin cushions, spools of colored thread, and needles could be found in homes as surely as bread and milk. Christmas dresses were sewn from Butterick and Simplicity patterns carefully pinned to fabric pieces. *Oh, what Mom couldn't create with a couple of yards of cloth—or from a ball of brightly-colored yarn!*

Who among us can't remember a pair of slippers—or a hat—crocheted by our grandmother during these simpler times? Or a sweater knitted by a favorite aunt who loved us very much—even if it was in our least favorite color? Or an afghan blanket made of "granny squares" fastened together with a crochet hook?

Often, these presents without price tags were the most heartfelt of all, and brought with them a sense of love and togetherness that material gains could not provide. These handmade gifts represented a personal investment of time by the giver, and you didn't need to worry about "batteries not included" or "assembly required." Truly, it was a period when many people

thought of a gift as something you made, not necessarily as something you bought.

No one knew the slogan "shop till you drop" because it didn't exist. Nor did plastic gift cards. Or purchases made on maxed-out credit cards. No one handed you a gift certificate and told you, "Go buy what you want." Times were different.

If you purchased a gift, you shopped in a building, not from a computer screen. (And stores weren't crowded, wall-to-wall, with people on December 26th asking for directions to the Refund-and-Exchange counter.)

Christmas. In days past, it meant a father sawing wood and a mother threading her needle, creating meaningful memories, despite an inability to provide store-bought items which sometimes had to remain on the shelves, unaffordable.

It was a time when there may not have been a lot of presents under the tree, but that didn't mean you didn't have gifts—even if your eyes couldn't see them. Gifts included love, family, devotion—and time. Time was a gift that was given not only at Christmas, but every day of the year; and you came to realize that the best things in life aren't wrapped inside pretty boxes with bows on top—they're held in your heart instead of your hand. It was a period in our nation's history when treasure was measured in terms of something that had nothing to do with money.

These financially-difficult years taught those who lived through them the value of thrift—and deferred gratification. People knew the satisfaction of sweat on their brow. These, too, were gifts—and they arrived unwrapped.

In the absence of high-tech physical entertainment, children came up with all sorts of creative ideas for free fun and enjoyment. There were hopscotch and marbles. And jumping rope. Checkerboards sat between excited players shouting, "King me!" Paper airplanes soared, and so did homemade kites! Pirate hats made from folded newspapers decorated the heads of three-foot-tall buccaneers. Boys and girls could be entertained by just about anything they could cut from a piece of paper!

And who could forget "Red Rover, Red Rover, Let Walter Come Over" and "Red Light, Green Light, Hope to See the Ghost Tonight"?

Little fingers created alligators and bunny rabbits made of shadows, hopping along white walls, while vivid imaginations outside saw giraffes, not clouds, float across blue skies. At night, you knew how to locate the Big Dipper, as well as a firefly.

And there was always time for a game of cards—"Go Fish" or "Crazy Eights." There was hardly an idle moment because a game of tag was usually just around the corner—or a baseball game. *Batter up!* You could dream you were Joe DiMaggio, Lou Gehrig or Babe Ruth playing under bright stadium lights for the whole game! Boys and girls had hopes as large as life, but they also displayed a contentedness between the dreaming and the coming true.

Yesterday. It included tackle boxes and fishing poles. And hammocks and porch swings. And tree houses and tire swings. And gratitude for the simplest things.

The 1950s came to a close with voices echoing "Ride 'em, cowboy!" and "All, aboard!" These were quickly replaced with other phrases like "Blast off!" as the 1960s inspired in little ones big dreams of daring space exploration. These words can almost be deemed symbolic of the period, as the changing times seemed to ignite the "launch" of a faster-paced society, leaving simple, old-fashioned Christmases to be cherished in the memories of those who experienced them.

There was real magic to be found in those moments, shared as a family and long remembered. Time would pass, and the children would grow older. And as those children inevitably made the transition into adulthood, their Christmas wish lists changed, as well. There were no longer desires for dolls and baseball mitts, but rather hopes of replicating the feelings of Christmases past, to re-live the subtle moments of happiness and offer their own touch of magic to the lives of a new generation of children which completed the now-larger family. And so the cycle of Christmas continued, as certain as the returning seasons, tradition passing through the changing years, and decades, and generations.

# City Sidewalks

'Mid roar of brass and beating drums,
The grand parade—see, here it comes!
Children screaming with delight,
Laughter, splendor—what a sight!

Christmas in New York City
R. H. Macy holiday parade advertisement

# City Sidewalks

Visiting the city, especially at Christmastime, was an event that was anticipated with great excitement. A certain awe sprang up when you witnessed the bustling center of metropolitan life transform into a sparkling, festive holiday wonderland.

Families traveled into the city from quiet, small-town communities, nestled among rolling hills. Often, a family's entire Christmas shopping list could be taken care of in a single visit. Children emptied their piggy banks, carefully counting and re-counting the mix of coins inside—silver dimes and copper "wheat" pennies. Housewives brought mason jars out of hiding places at the back of pantry cupboards—jars filled with single dollar bills tucked neatly inside, saved one by one.

Brightly-lit Christmas decorations adorned the high-reaching tops of light poles along city sidewalks, illuminating block after block with heartwarming symbols of the season. Horns honked, and broad downtown lanes filled with the ceaseless motion of automobiles steering over trolley tracks and past train depots.

Sidewalks came alive with throngs of shoppers—men in pants, and women in dresses. Overcoats thickened to shield passers-by against winter winds that wove between tall buildings. Autumn-colored scarves were

**Bundle-carrying shoppers**
CHICAGO, 1936

replaced with those of red and green, displaying personal expressions of holiday cheer.

Voices filled the air, and shoppers greeted one another on crowded streets, exchanging smiles. These were "the good old days," when a gentleman tipped his hat when approaching a lady, and offered a handshake to fellows.  Men held doors open for the opposite gender and pulled out chairs before women were seated.

Corner diners served pots of coffee faster than they could be brewed, and from your spot at the counter, you could sometimes catch a whiff of the sweet-smelling tobacco smoke rolling off an old man's smoldering pipe.

A quick blast of heat could be felt as revolving department store doors twirled shoppers—with brightly-colored packages tucked snugly beneath their close-drawn arms—in from the street.

Yes, what a feeling to be in the city at Christmastime! Downtown seemed a magical world that only surfaced into existence once-a-year. Christmas tunes poured from gigantic department store speakers. Signs in storefronts read "14 Days until Christmas," increasing anticipation. Families strolled along streets, walking from window to window, shopping with their eyes. Toy shops. Hat boutiques. Pet stores—with cuddly critters peeking out from behind the panes, waiting to be taken home. Children raced ahead and pressed hands and noses against the glass, surveying the wondrous scenes inside, dreaming of the special gift they were hoping to find beneath the tree—a shiny new bike with a silver bell mounted to the handlebar, or a spotted puppy.

Merchants boxed your purchases—and then wrapped your selections, too. Thick rolls of decorative paper were mounted to countertops for a complimentary service to shoppers. Excellent service extended to every department of the store, not just the check-out line. Clerks took time to measure your feet in the shoe department to ensure you were purchasing the appropriate size. Clothing departments staffed seamstresses to accommodate necessary alterations—guaranteeing a tailored-fit garment. And a visit to the candy counter meant flavorful favorites could be chosen by the piece—or by the whole handful. Lemon drops, peppermint sticks, nutty fudge, and chocolate-covered cherries were all carefully weighed on confectionary scales.

Outside, street-side movie theaters on city sidewalks displayed holiday film titles on lighted marquees protruding from building faces.

*Did you know . . .*

*It's a Wonderful Life* was a box office disappointment. Although the movie was nominated for five Academy Awards, it failed to make the top 25 grossing films for 1947. (Even though the film underachieved at its release, it is still considered one of the great films of the twentieth century.)

*Sesame Street's* "Bert and Ernie" were named after Bert, the police officer, and Ernie, the taxi driver, in *It's a Wonderful Life.*

Although the movie portrayed life in the 1920s and 1930s, the film's writers made an "oooops" in three scenes, forgetting it was illegal to manufacture or sell liquor in the United States between 1920 and 1933. (It was even illegal to drink a beer!)

1. Harry announced to his folks that he planned to drink gin on graduation night.
2. Employees at the Building and Loan opened a bottle of liquor in celebration after they were able to survive the bank run.
3. George and Mary were gifted a bottle of champagne for their wedding by Bert—*the police officer!!*

FRANK CAPRA'S

# It's a Wonderful Life

Many Main Street memories were made in the grand theaters of yesterday for a ten-cent admission price. Several classic Christmas films debuted on the big screen in decades past including *A Christmas Carol* in the 1930s, *It's a Wonderful Life* and *Miracle on 34th Street* in the 1940s, and *White Christmas* in the 1950s. Films like these have become as much a part of Christmas as holly and berries, and perhaps even more so.

These were the days when movie-goers were treated to a bit of organ music from a mighty Wurlitzer prior to the start of the show. But once the reel of film started flickering, audience members knew that they had better not make a peep because ushers kept order during evening showings and afternoon matinees. If you saw their flashlight beam coming down the aisle, you knew you had better hush—or else!

Newspaper vendors could be found on busy street corners shouting, "Read all about it!" Many of these daily publications sold for a nickel or less, and annually re-printed the much-loved "Yes, Virginia, there is a Santa Claus" letter to commemorate the season. Other newspapers included the best-known poem in the English language for their readers' enjoyment— "Twas the Night Before Christmas."

Street corners were shared by Salvation Army volunteers who collected donations on behalf of the down-trodden. A lengthy ringing of bells urged passers-by to be charitable with those in need. Coins dropped into the red metal kettles with a "clink" meant extra mouths would receive a hot meal for Christmas. Salvation Army bands were also a familiar institution on city corners, as well as in parades, through the 1950s, with the

**"The World's Largest Stocking"**
**NEW YORK CITY, 1937**

steady beat of their boots pulsing in sync with their instruments.

Laughter echoed from street-side parks as skaters carved circles in city ice-rinks. Couples sat on wooden benches, gazing upward at half-lit buildings against a backdrop of starry skies. Christmas decorations lined the walkways of parks, and with the help of snowy landscapes, created what seemed like a new world in which to momentarily escape daily life.

Once a year, in almost every city, came the day, or evening, of the long-awaited Christmas parade. Crowds swelled. Dozens of floats, carefully planned and decorated by commercial businesses and community organizations, gathered at an assembly point where brass bands were lined up in smart formation. Then, a whistle was blown and the parade proceeded down the center of Main Street.

High school marching bands proudly offered their musical talents behind wide banners displaying their school's mascot. Uniformed members marched in musical step behind conductors with raised batons. Trumpets sounded, and drums, too, drawing applause every step of the way.

Onlookers squeezed together along curbs lining both sides of the street, huddling close in the crisp, cold air. An ever-so-light blanket of snow would sometimes sprinkle down, decorating the tops of woolen hats with a dusting of white. Spectators could also be seen peering through apartment windows high above the lively scene below.

The fame of the annual Macy's parade in New York City superseded all parades. Mammoth balloons bobbed up and down the pavement. Countless onlookers greeted the high-flying drama with cheers as each balloon came into view. Parade-watchers in seventh-story windows along the route went eye-to-eye with these visual spectacles which were secured by long ropes held fast by men with childlike hearts.

Children along curbsides shivered with ear-to-ear smiles as they watched the procession of baton twirlers and costumed characters marching in evenly-paced steps—clowns, elves and popular fictional personalities of

the day—hoping to be given a piece of candy or two. Some youngsters were perched on top of their father's shoulders for a privileged view. The attention of children was not drawn from the lively scene—not even for a moment. Their little eyes were glued to the passing line of holiday enchantment as if real magic were taking place in their very presence, and if they were to look away—or even blink—the whole of it might disappear.

Everyone eagerly awaited the parade's perennial grand finale—the famed red sleigh carrying Santa Claus himself, safely secured to the top of a trailer. Reindeer, with branch-like antlers, were harnessed to the sleigh, adding to the thrill of wee ones lining the route. "Look, Daddy!" shouted youngsters. "It's Santa Claus!"

Old Saint Nick was certainly the ultimate crowd-pleaser—and the most recognizable face of the day. A wave from the Master Toymaker's hand drew hoots and hollers—and ooooohs and aaaaahs—from the crowd, and kiddies felt Santa was waving directly at them. "He waved at me!" they shouted to mothers and fathers. "Santa waved at me!"

A few brave souls scurried into the street, arms outstretched and waving a letter postmarked for the North Pole, in hopeful expectation of hand-delivering the urgent document.

Slowly, the procession moved forward, onward to more anxious families further down the street. Eyes followed Santa until he faded from view, and the jolly sound of his "ho ho ho" could no longer be heard. At that moment it seemed to grow just a little bit chillier, as if the generous-hearted Kris Kringle had brought with him a communal warmth for all of

**"Hi, Santa!"**
**Christmas parade, 1943, Milwaukee, Wisconsin**

mankind, which followed him down the street.

Then, as the storefront lights flickered out, the crowd made its way past the misty halos of lit lampposts, back to wherever they called "home," satisfied with the night's festivities. They tucked themselves into warm beds, comforted to sleep by the feeling that is Christmas.

Cathy Stern

# I'll Be Home for Christmas

"Christmas Eve will find me
where the love-light gleams.
I'll be home for Christmas,
if only in my dreams.

KIM GANNON and WALTER KENT, 1943

# I'll Be Home for Christmas

This Christmas, as you read these pages, it is likely that you will be surrounded by those dearest to you—with fathers, brothers, sons, and nephews close by. Take them not for granted, for merely two generations ago, Christmas marked a trying time for most families—a time of sacrifice and endurance—a time when many faces were missing. These were the Christmases of World War II, and this chapter is about those years.

President Roosevelt declared war shortly before Christmas 1941 with the following words: "Yesterday, December 7, 1941—a date which will live in infamy—the United States of America was suddenly and deliberately attacked by naval and air forces of the empire of Japan."

The President's words changed the lives of millions over the next several years, dividing families. A complete upheaval of American society followed the announcement.

The United States participated in the worldwide conflict from 1941 until 1945. It was a war that ultimately claimed the lives of over 54 million persons—an incomprehensible number. Many soldiers were unable to spend a single Christmas with their loved ones during this period.

Six million Americans volunteered to serve in World War II and enlisted on their own, accepting Uncle Sam's urging: "I want *you!*"

Ten million more were inducted into service through the draft. Draftees included single men and married men—and fathers. Men between the ages of twenty-one and thirty-six were initially required to register, but as the military ranks grew thin, the breadth of the draft registration spanned men from eighteen years of age all the way up to sixty-five. Young

Christmas Greetings

**Vintage Christmas card**

fellows who unwrapped baseball bats and Monopoly games underneath Christmas trees only a single year prior were now considered "men" and ordered into neat, buttoned-down uniforms, boarding outbound trains and buses destined for faraway battlefields.

The holiday season of 1941 came before most were forced to ship out to fight, so there was still time for one more "almost normal Christmas" before the difficult years began.  The memory of peaceful holidays helped carry soldiers through the less-than-comfortable Christmases that soon transpired—celebrations that were not red and green, but rather red, white and blue.  The Christmases of World War II were more about duty, honor, country and sacrifice than they were about wrapping paper, evergreen trees, and the North Pole.

Empty trains pulled into towns, and loved ones said their emotional goodbyes at depot stations. Fathers gave sons parting handshakes.  Lovers embraced in a final kiss. Teary-eyed mothers hugged boys they had given life to. Those same trains, filled with as many able-bodied men as they could hold, rolled out, leaving behind only a dissipating cloud of steam, hovering over bare tracks.  Whistles sounded in the distance, as if to echo a last farewell to those still standing at the edge of the platform, gazing out.

These scenes were only the beginning of what families—and an entire nation—endured.  Mothers wished their sons would come home safely almost immediately after they departed.  Family members on the homefront listened intently and nervously to every detailed report of the conflict transmitted over radio broadcasts as they paced back and forth. President Roosevelt attempted to ease fears with regular broadcasts to the public.  His "fireside chats" began with the words "My fellow Americans" or "Good evening, friends," and his calm, confident voice proved to be a steady pulse for the nation.  (President and Mrs. Roosevelt knew, first hand, the pain of being separated from loved ones.  Four of their own sons served in World War II.)

# "WE'VE ENLISTED!"

# THERE WILL BE

# NO PARADE

Maps of Europe were hung on kitchen walls by mothers and fathers, and attempts were made to locate distant places, far from home—locations they couldn't even pronounce. It was a way to keep abreast of battles as the latest news from the frontlines became available. Family members desperately tried to grasp the geography a son, father or brother trekked.

Flags were hung in front windows of homes, displaying blue stars. Each star represented one family member serving their country. If a blue star was replaced by a gold star, it meant your loved one had perished.

World War II became expensive quickly and brought lean years for those on the homefront. An unprecedented shortage of food and supplies made it necessary for the U.S. government to impose rations. Shortages during the war included coffee, butter, cheese, meat, shortening, canned

## Did you know . . .

The Macy's parade was cancelled in 1942, 1943, and 1944 during World War II due to a rubber shortage. (Rubber was a rationed commodity needed for the war effort.) Macy's donated all of their rubber helium balloons to the U.S. government in 1942. The balloons were melted down and manufactured into tires for tanks, and life-rafts for naval sailors. The parade returned in 1945 after the war ended with a new collection of balloons.

The R. H. Macy and Company parade was originally called the "Macy's Christmas Parade" for ten years. The name was then changed to the "Macy's Santa Claus Parade." Today, it is known as the "Macy's Thanksgiving Day Parade."

The colossal balloons used during earlier parades were released at the end of the parade. Rewards in the amount of $100.00 were offered for the return of each balloon. The balloons were timed with a slow leak before they were set free so they would stay afloat for at least one week. The balloon releases were discontinued in 1933 after two mishaps involving airplanes.

Macy's in New York City was the largest department store in the world during the 1930s, 1940s, and 1950s. Marshall Field's in Chicago was the second largest retail department store, and Harrod's in London was the third.

goods, and sugar. Families planted "victory" gardens—*twenty million of them!*—to help supplement the food supply. Other shortages included fabric, clothes, and shoes, as well as coal, rubber, plastic, and heating oil. These were some of the products in desperate need, not only for soldiers fighting in foreign trenches, but for factories building war supplies, as well. The manufacturing of many consumer luxuries, such as new automobiles, came to a halt, their assembly lines diverted to the production of trucks, planes, tanks, and bombs.

"Fill 'er up" became a phrase of memory, as fuel rations left every gas tank shallow. Most people walked everywhere they could, or rode their bike.

With set rations, Americans were forced to adjust their habits. They ate less (or more) of certain foods. Rationed food was eaten more slowly so it would last longer. Americans drove less, and even drove more slowly. With only four gallons of gasoline allotted to each individual per week, the national speed limit was reduced to forty miles per hour to preserve the precious fuel further. (The gas ration was later lowered to three gallons. Christmas visits were cancelled if the trip required more than that.)

Ladies did not wear nylons to Christmas parties during World War II because pantyhose and silk stockings were also in short supply. (These items were collected and sewn into parachutes and gun powder bags.)

Milkweed pods were collected from fields and ditches so the fluffy white seeds inside could be used to stuff life preservers.

Metal was in such short supply that the production of new appliances was halted. (The production of new homes was also halted.) Empty cans

## Pedal Power

**Americans rode their bikes everywhere they could—or walked—during the gas rationing years of World War II.**

**There's No Thrill Like His First Christmas with LIONEL TRAINS**

and scrap metal were collected at recycling drives. Paper, lumber, and steel were also collected.

Production of Lionel trains stopped. (The metal was needed for the war effort.) The U.S. government regulated conveyor lines, restricting the manufacture of many goods, including new bicycles. The government determined "what was needed and who would produce it." Trains and bicycles were two of many items removed from "Dear Santa" letters during World War II. (The purchase of a new bike required special permission from the rationing board.)

Children weren't alone in amending their Christmas lists. Soldiers, aching for the comfort of home, wished for "a good meal, a glass of milk, a haircut by a barber, a tiled bathroom with hot and cold water, a bed with springs and clean sheets, a plush-lined trench, a 60-day furlough with their wife and children" and, of course, "an end to the war."

American soldiers, scattered around the globe, yearned to return to

their own beds, under the same roofs as their families. They spent their nights dreaming of "the thoughts, the feelings, the sights, and the smells of home" as they gazed upward at the twilight. Some found comfort in the thought that loved ones back home looked up at the same starry skies. Soldiers closed their eyes and suddenly they weren't an ocean away from those they cared about, but in their midst, home again, "if only in their dreams." Christmas reunions were both "real and imagined," with many of these reunions taking place only in hearts and minds.

> "Christmas may be a day of feasting, or a day of prayer, but always it will be a day of remembrance—a day on which we think of everyone we have ever loved."
>
> **AUGUSTA RUNDEL**

Those fighting in tropical locations missed the snow as they marched on during those hot, humid Christmases. Others in northern trenches, with frozen fingers and limbs, missed the warmth of a family-room fireplace.

Although the troops were unable to experience the luxuries of home firsthand, they could gain a bit of satisfaction through long-written descriptions in letters arriving from the States. The postal service proved to be the most important communication device between soldiers and their families during the long and brutally-lonely war years. It was a time before the internet, e-mails, and cellular telephones, making communication difficult and time-consuming. Many unfortunate captives even sent word from behind the barbed-wire gates of P.O.W. camps in an attempt to comfort worried loved ones back home.

Packages and gifts sent overseas for Christmas were the only link between soldiers and their families during the holiday if a furlough had not been granted. Folks back home shipped their gifts plenty early so they would make it to—well, dots on a map most people had never heard of.

Copies of local newspapers were shipped to those stationed in far-off places. Nothing quite told of life back in your neighborhood like hometown headlines and photos taken by local reporters. Though thousands of physical miles distant, a soldier—in his heart and mind—felt as if he were back; and there was no feeling in the world quite like reaching for the doorknob attached to the front door of your home, even if it could only be in a passing thought.

Although a large number of citizens were abroad—both men and women serving as soldiers and nurses—life on the homefront went on. Radios blared with *The Adventures of Ozzie and Harriet* and *The Roy Rogers Show.* Carolers sang *Jingle Bells.* Bing Crosby recorded *White Christmas.* Gifts were purchased and wrapped—even though there was a paper shortage. (Bottles of perfume were wrapped in hankies, and kitchen items were wrapped in embroidered towels. Gift-givers were creative in their packaging choices.)

At times, Christmas took a toll, requiring great effort to force a happy holiday, which was evident in the music and print media of the time, like Bing Crosby's recording, *I'll Be Home for Christmas.* Families gathered

> **"Home—our feet may leave, but never our hearts."**
>
> **OLIVER WENDELL HOLMES**

## A Christmas furlough during World War II

around tables to celebrate, although empty chairs were quiet reminders of missing faces. It was a sacrifice of separation.

Families, though thinner than usual, met and celebrated as best they could, with children and stockings and toys and cookies. The magic was not lost, just temporarily displaced.

Besides a lack of goods, there happened another obvious shortage—a shortage of men. As the male population was deployed and shipped off to serve on battlefields, factories began to fill their assembly lines with women. Ladies, laboring tirelessly, took on roles in production previously reserved only for the masculine members of society. "We're all in this together" was a common phrase of World War II. Efforts were united for victory—whether those efforts were on the frontlines or in a non-combative way. The "army back home" served in manufacturing plants and on ration boards. These "soldiers without uniforms" included kids collecting metal scraps and people buying war bonds with every coin they could spare. (The war was largely financed by members of society, both adults and children, who voluntarily gave the government their money in exchange for a war bond—a promise made by the government to pay the money back with interest. Many employees deducted a ten-percent dollar amount every week from their paycheck for a war bond purchase. The program was a remarkably successful means of raising capital for war efforts.)

With a lack of men, women needed to adjust to running a household alone, which popularized such books as *So, Your Husband's Gone to War* and *The Navy Wife*. The simple act of waiting—enduring unending days of unmatched loneliness—was considered a feat of individual courage. Suffering went beyond the battlefield—it was personal, as well.

Female Santas appeared in department stores, although they received considerable resistance at first. Many people felt it was taking the gender replacement practice a bit too far.

Christmases abroad were certainly nothing compared to the longed-for celebrations back home. Some soldiers were more fortunate than others in their holiday experiences, dining on special mess-hall meals on Christmas Eve and singing carols by candlelight. Others made due with what they had, eating the same monotonous meal they had eaten the day prior, the same meal they would eat the next day. Military personnel huddled together in foxholes and inhospitable trenches dug into the frost-hardened European soil, safe from the whizzing bullets overhead. Fighting knew no holiday.

Soldiers stationed away from frontlines decorated their shelters with makeshift Christmas trees and trimmed them with ornaments cut from flattened tin cans and package-wrappings taken from food rations. Doctors and nurses used rubber gloves as ornaments on their trees in the hope of bringing a little cheer to the dismal scene of wounded men dying in the season of peace.

Back home, loved ones continued to make Christmas wishes that had nothing to do with shopping bags. They wished for the battle to end, and they wished for their sons, brothers, and fathers to remain "safe and sound" and "warm and dry" until that time arrived. Homecomings were longed for—not just for Christmas, but for good.

Eventually, many of these wishes came true, but the nature of war would not allow all of them to. Countless soldiers who served did not return, and the lives of their family members were changed forever.

Those who survived boarded crowded trains so they could arrive home by Christmas where their loved ones were waiting, the same loved ones who had kissed them goodbye years earlier. They were now ready to hug and kiss them hello—not with an "X" or an "O" written at the end of a letter, but for real.

Steam whistles blew, and the most treasured gifts of Christmas 1945 were exchanged on depot platforms.

**The homecoming**

# Fa La La La La

"Let's dance and sing and make good cheer,
for Christmas comes but once a year."

**SIR GEORGE ALEXANDER MACFARREN**

# *Fa La La La La*

What makes Christmas Christmas?   Surely, the sounds of the season herald in the holiday as much as the scents and sights.  A snatch of a favorite tune is all it takes to know—and hear—Christmas is on its way.  "Fa la la la la," "pa-rum-pum-pum-pum," and "a partridge in a pear tree."

To some folks, Christmas just wouldn't be Christmas without singing *Silent Night* and *Away in the Manger,* or *Jingle Bells* and *Santa Claus is Coming to Town.*  We have come to expect these once-a-year songs as the holiday nears.  We hum along—or give voice to memorized lyrics. *"Dashing through the snow, in a one-horse open sleigh!"*

Many of today's most loved carols were born during the years between 1930 and 1960.  This period ushered in the Golden Age of Christmas music. Songs recorded during this time have brought yuletide cheer to family celebrations around the country—and even the world—season after season.

It was also the Golden Age of radio, an era which spanned from 1920 through the mid-1950s.  Radio was the favorite means of family entertainment—*static and all!*—until televisions became more available and affordable after the mid-century point.

Listeners adjusted their tuning knobs ever-so-slightly, an eighth of

# It's Beginning to Sound a Lot Like Christmas

| | | |
|---|---|---|
| 1934 | Santa Claus is Coming to Town | *George Hall* |
| 1934 | Winter Wonderland | *Guy Lombardo* |
| 1942 | White Christmas | *Bing Crosby* |
| 1943 | I'll Be Home for Christmas | *Bing Crosby* |
| 1944 | Have Yourself a Merry Little Christmas | *Judy Garland* |
| 1945 | Let it Snow! Let it Snow! Let it Snow! | *Vaughn Monroe* |
| 1946 | The Christmas Song (Chestnuts Roasting) | *Nat King Cole* |
| 1947 | Here Comes Santa Claus | *Gene Autry* |
| 1948 | All I Want for Christmas is My Two Front Teeth | *Spike Jones* |
| 1949 | Rudolph the Red-Nosed Reindeer | *Gene Autry* |
| 1949 | Sleigh Ride | *Arthur Fiedler* |
| 1949 | Baby, It's Cold Outside | *Dinah Shore* |
| 1950 | Frosty the Snowman | *Gene Autry* |
| 1951 | It's Beginning to Look a Lot Like Christmas | *Perry Como* |
| 1952 | Silver Bells | *Bing Crosby* |
| 1952 | I Saw Mommy Kissing Santa Claus | *Jimmy Boyd* |
| 1953 | Santa, Baby | *Eartha Kitt* |
| 1954 | There's No Place Like Home for the Holidays | *Perry Como* |
| 1955 | I'm Getting Nuttin' for Christmas | *Barry Gordon* |
| 1957 | Jingle Bell Rock | *Bobby Helms* |
| 1957 | Blue Christmas | *Elvis Presley* |
| 1958 | Rockin' Around the Christmas Tree | *Brenda Lee* |
| 1958 | The Little Drummer Boy | *Harry Simeone Chorale* |

**SANTA CLAUS IS COMIN' TO TOWN**

(J. Fred Coots-Haven Gillespie)

Sung by BOBBY NICHOLAS

with the Peter Pan Orchestra and Chorus

Directed by Vicky Kasen

X-6 A

NON-BREAKABLE
(With Normal Use)

PETER PAN RECORDS

MFR'D. BY SYNTHETIC PLASTICS CO., NEWARK, N. J., U.S.A.

a turn to the right, then back just a bit to the left, then slightly more to the right, alternating between static and voice, static and voice. Once tuned in, radio programming offered commentary and comedy, mystery and romance, adventure and thrillers, sports broadcasts, game shows, news bulletins, farm reports, weather forecasts and, of course, music.

Listeners knew the names of those who performed the memorable tunes of the 1930s, 1940s and 1950s—whether in voice or in band. They knew who Irving Berlin was, and Glenn Miller, too. They knew Duke Ellington, Benny Goodman, Tommy Dorsey, and Louis Armstrong. And Danny Kaye and Doris Day.

And who could forget The Andrew Sisters? Or Burl Ives? Or Jimmy Durante, Gene Autry, and Bob Hope? Or Ella Fitzgerald and Judy Garland?

*Did you know . . .*

**The first radio broadcast occurred on Christmas Eve, 1906. The voice transmitted over the airways was that of Reginald Fessenden, a 33-year-old university professor in Pittsburgh and former Chief Chemist for Thomas Edison. He read the Biblical Christmas story from the Gospel of Luke: "And she brought forth her firstborn son, and wrapped him in swaddling clothes, and laid him in a manger, because there was no room for them in the inn." When the reading was complete, Fessenden picked up his violin and played "O Holy Night," the first song ever sent over radio waves.**

# Fa La La La La

Or the velvety voices of Nat King Cole, Perry Como, Andy Williams, and Dean Martin? Folks who lived through this era can remember these names as well as they can remember their own. These performers defined the holiday musically, and their's were the songs listeners came to expect during those long-ago days when crowding around a radio was a familiar feeling—at Christmas and otherwise.

Radio listeners recognized the Shadow's spooky voice, and the Lone Ranger shouting, "Hi, Ho, Silver, and away!" They smiled when Shirley Temple sang about her good ship, *Lollipop.* And they laughed with Groucho Marx, Milton Berle, and Red Skelton. And Amos and Andy—and Abbott and Costello, too. These voices were "part of the family" because they were heard regularly in living rooms across the country after supper.

There was time for radio listening, and there was time for music. Most importantly, there was time for each other. People even danced! (Not quite as well as Ginger Rogers and Fred Astaire, but they sure did try!)

Folks knew how to waltz and how to swing dance. They could do the Charleston, the Lindy Hop, and the Jitterbug. Big band orchestras—with trumpets and trombones and saxophones—filled dance halls to their limit with spirited music. (Toes were stepped on, but it didn't matter; those memories wouldn't be traded today for anything in the world.) People knew how to "do the hokey pokey and turn themselves around" because that's what it was all about. *Aaahhh, music!* There's nothing quite like it for brightening a spirit—and most especially at Christmas!

As the holiday approached, music took its hold. Church basements began filling with choir members seated on wooden folding chairs scattered around an upright piano, sheet music in hand. Special yuletide melodies were chosen by directors long in advance of those weeknight practices. Congregations could be certain to hear "Hallelujah!" and "Rejoice!" from robed singers on Christmas Eve trying to express in song what happened at the miracle birth long ago.

At local schools, students practiced holiday songs for their annual concert during the weeks that led up to Christmas, while band members rehearsed favorites on tubas, flutes, clarinets, and drums, perfecting their notes.

And who can forget the sound of carolers' voices, strung together

in unison, outside your front door? It wasn't such a long time ago that Christmas carolers were as much a part of the holiday as fruit cake. There really was something special about the tradition, whether you only listened, or carried a booklet of songs with you, proceeding from house to house with a musical greeting: *"We wish you a merry Christmas, we wish you a merry Christmas, we wish you a merry Christmas, and a Happy New Year!"*

These sounds heralded the holiday. Christmas meant carolers standing on welcome mats outside front doors, joining their voices to enter a song, and it meant school programs filled with pageantry—children innocently singing off-key, like the youngster who proudly announced to his teacher, "I'm not a good singer, but I am loud."

Christmas meant choirs climbing into formation on tiered risers, harmonizing in tones of soprano, alto, tenor, and bass, and it meant families gathered at home making music together on accordions and harmonicas, singing *"Oh, Tannenbaum"* and *"Stille Nacht"* in a grandparent's native tongue. It was a time of merry-making and foot tapping.

It meant radio broadcasts of the old favorites in December—Perry Como singing *There's No Place Like Home for the Holidays* and Gene Autry singing *Rudolph the Red-Nosed Reindeer.* Radio was enjoyed all year, but never so much as it was during the Christmas season.

And who could forget the family record player and the scratchy discs that spun around and around, the needle following a grooved path carved into the plastic?

Christmas. Our memories of having "heard" it in yuletides past

remained with us long after the moments did.

Even the bestselling Christmas song of all time, Bing Crosby's *White Christmas,* is a nostalgic glance backward. Its lyrics—*"I'm dreaming of a white Christmas, just like the ones I used to know"*—beckon the remembrance of bygone holidays.

*Did you know . . .*

The song *White Christmas* was first performed by Bing Crosby on December 25, 1941, and the movie—starring Bing Crosby, Danny Kaye, Rosemary Clooney, and Vera Ellen—followed in 1954.

*White Christmas* remained the world's best-selling song for over 50 years.

Bing Crosby produced more recordings than any other singer in history, and also achieved more number-one hits during his career—*38 total!* (The Beatles recorded 24 number-one hits; Elvis Presley recorded 18.)

Bing Crosby's real name was Harry Lillis Crosby.

# Oh, Christmas Tree

"Each year, we'd hike out to the timber to select our tree. The older boys would cut the tree, bring it home and anchor it in a milk pail.  Mama would give us an old white sheet to drape around the pail as a tree skirt.  Then it was time to make our decorations. We'd settle in at the dining room table, with the kerosene lamp glowing in the middle.  We always thought our tree was the most beautiful tree ever—even with the smeared paste that showed on our paper chains."

EDNA HULON

# Oh, Christmas Tree

Flipping through the yellowing pages of vintage photo albums is a nostalgic visit back in time to Christmas as it used to be. Old photos of smiling families posed in front of their Christmas tree capture the spirit of Christmas past in flash-bulb snapshots.

The Christmas tree, or "tannenbaum" as it was often called, has long been central to the celebration of the holiday, having endured as a seasonal cornerstone through decades. And although the tradition of tree trimming has remained primarily the same, photographs reveal subtle changes made during passing generations—real candles decorated branches during the 1930s *(and the candles were actually lit!)*, newly-invented bubble lights were favored in the 1940s, and large, multi-colored bulbs were a popular choice of the 1950s.

As December neared, and the thermometer's thin red line dipped into single digits (and sometimes below), neighborhoods were decorated with wreaths and boughs—a festive array of greenery to herald the season. Christmas was coming, and it was time to rearrange the furniture in order to make room for the fresh-cut tree that would soon be on its way. Staring at the empty space where the new tree would stand, you could almost imagine the subtle scent of pine.

# Christmas Lights
## by NOMA

The heavy, metal tree-stand was sought for in the dusty attic, or from the rafters above the garage. Then, the holiday tree-skirt was located, carefully pressed, and made ready for the presents that would soon be stacked high upon it beneath the outstretched branches of the tree. There they'd lie untouched, awaiting their opening on Christmas morning.

While many trees were purchased from vendors on street corners, the true heart of Christmas could still be found in the tradition of cutting your own tree, with your own hands, on a tree farm or from your family's ancestral land. It was a tradition that was eagerly anticipated—with the knowledge that the act of erecting the family tree was an important chapter in the holiday season. The evergreen was more than a decoration—it was a cherished symbol. And for most people of the time, the idea of pulling an artificial Christmas tree out of a box was as difficult to imagine as a fit-and-trim Santa Claus or Rudolph with a blue nose—it could hardly be done! Celebrating the holiday with a "real" Christmas tree was worth the trouble, even if it meant getting sap on your hands—which took days to scrub away—and finding pine needles in July, still threaded into the carpeting, giving small pricks to unsuspecting toes.

Mothers bundled their children in snowsuits, with scarves wrapped round and round, and fathers sharpened the blades of their saws. Excited family members set out for the wintry woods, following Dad, who carried an axe over his shoulder or the saw in his hand. With snow up to their ankles—or knees!—everyone trudged forward in search of a tree to fill that empty space.

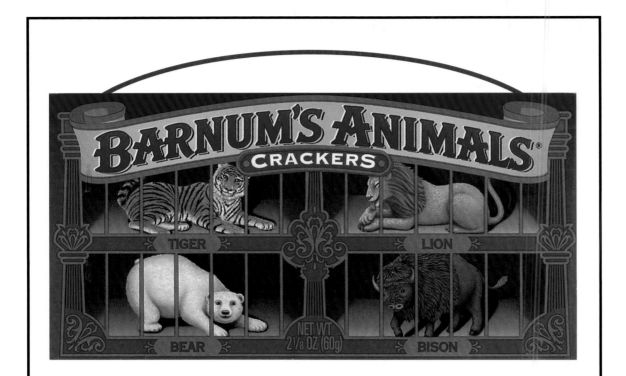

**The National Biscuit Company attached a handle to packages of animal crackers so the box could be used as a Christmas tree ornament.**

Picking the perfect tree was something of an art. It was an important decision, and required the keen skills of each member of the family. A good tree must first be identified from afar. Everyone, eager at the thought that this might be "the one," rushed forward and gathered around the tower of green branches. Then came the measurements. The only "tools" used to make these calculations were the heights of fathers and sons, compared to their memory of the room back home where the tree would eventually take residence. And, of course, it was necessary for mothers and daughters to examine the tree from all sides, making a visual assessment, checking for open spaces—"bald spots"—and gaps between the branches. Upon completion of this careful analysis, the tree would either be chosen, or the quest would continue.

Finally, after searching, measuring, and touching every branch, the selection of the perfect Christmas tree was complete. The sharp teeth of Dad's saw cut through the bark of the trunk, sprinkling the white snow

## Did you know . . .

Electric Christmas tree lights were invented in 1882 by Edward Johnson, an associate of Thomas Edison. The colored bulbs were hand-painted and hand-wired.

The Rockefeller Center Christmas tree tradition began in New York City in 1931.

According to *The Guinness Book of World Records*, the tallest Christmas tree ever cut was a 221-foot Douglas fir. The tree was erected in Seattle, Washington, in December, 1950.

with a yellowish tint of sawdust. The pine then fell with a soft thud as it landed on the fluffy ground.

The fresh evergreen bounced along against its spring-like branches as it was pulled back to the car. Then, with a bit of twine or rope, it was fastened to the vehicle's roof, or laid in the back of an old pickup truck.

Once home, a cup of warm cider was sometimes needed to thaw chilled fingers and toes before the tree was carried into the house.

The base of the trunk was sawed off, leaving a healthy chunk of wood to be used as the yule log during the following year. The log from the previous year's Christmas tree would be burned in the fireplace, according to tradition, during the holiday celebration.

The time then came for the tree to travel through the front door and be hoisted into an upright position, its base placed squarely in the stand. Metal screws were tightened after everyone made sure to give their say concerning whether the tree was straight or crooked. Once everyone agreed on the "correct" positioning of the tree—or most everyone—it was time to add the decorations. Not too surprisingly, it seemed the tree always ended up just a little bit lopsided—tilted slightly to the left, or to the right—yet beautiful.

Shiny round bulbs, both large and small, were carefully removed from protective ornament boxes sectioned into individual spaces. Small cellophane windows on box tops allowed you to view the keepsakes inside. They gleamed red, green, silver and gold. Youngsters, taking a closer look, were delighted to see their image reflected on an ornament's surface, their

face stretched by the curve of the shiny glass sphere.

Tinsel was hung from the ends of branches, and popcorn strings or linked paper chains spiraled from the very tip-top of the tree, down to the widening circle of spreading limbs at the tree's base. The oldest of the children was granted the privilege, the honor, of climbing the stepladder upward and lifting the star into place, its highest point nearly touching the ceiling.

Family members, in turn, picked their favorite decorations and ornaments, and hung them ever-so-gently on the ends of delicate branches. There were so many varieties! Glass and paper, shiny and dull, round and flat, big and small. Store-bought and homemade, new ones and old ones—some of which belonged to grandparents who carried them across the ocean when they migrated to America from Europe in earlier years. And, of course, among the most special, were those ornaments which were handmade by the children, crafted from pipe-cleaners and yarn scraps, perfect childhood expressions of Christmas cheer.

For the remainder of the season, the full evergreen, its branches sparkling with the unique, decorative touch of the family that chose it so carefully, would stand proud, offering all those who visited a glow of the holiday spirit. Each night, just before the children made their way up the stairs to the warmth of their beds, they would take one last look at the lighted tree, and their eyes would shine just as brightly.

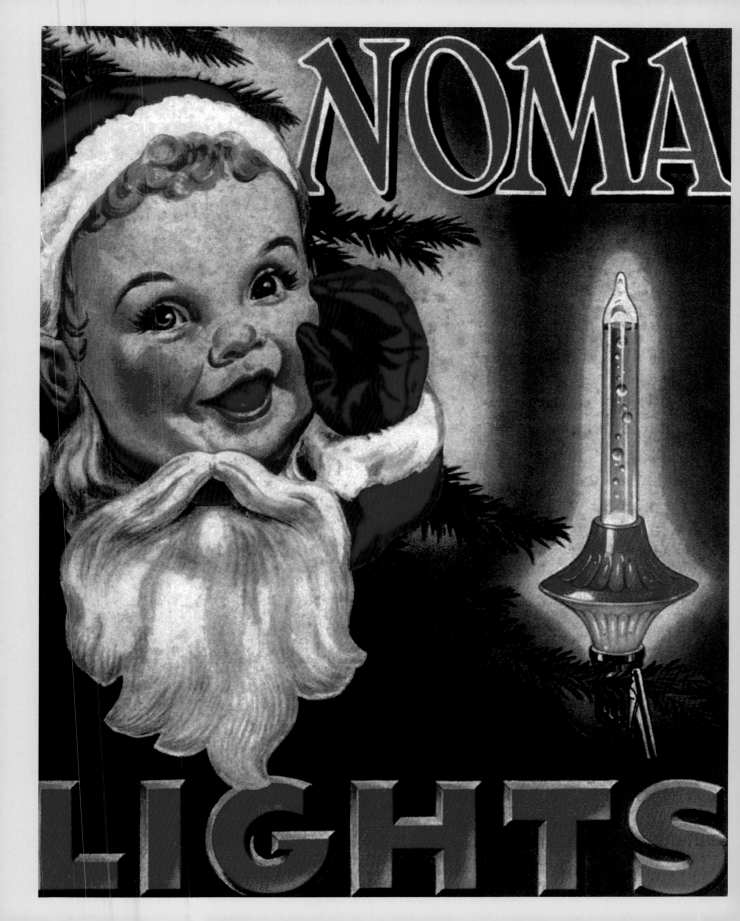

Cathy Stern

# Gathered Around the Table

"My tongue is smiling."

**ABIGAIL TRILLIN**

# Gathered Around the Table

Can you remember the smell of fresh-baked bread?  Or the taste of a flaky pie crust, served golden brown?  How about the gurgle of a percolating coffee pot?

This was a time before "fast food" and "coffee to go," a time when you sat down at the kitchen table to enjoy your meal, and if you traveled anywhere with a fresh-brewed cup of coffee, it was only as far as the front porch.  It was a time when front porches were for sitting on, not just for decoration.

Food was served on dishes made of glass, and your "fast food" choices were limited to such things as an oven-baked cookie pulled from beneath the lid of a countertop jar, a peanut butter and jelly sandwich you made yourself, or maybe a ripe, juicy apple picked from a tree that grew within sight of your backyard window.

Nothing about food preparation went quickly.  Breads were baked from scratch, vegetables were grown in your own garden and later canned, and double-layered cakes originated from a flour bin, not from a box.

It was a time when a "dishwasher" was not a machine, it was a person—or several people pitching in to divide the chore of cleaning up the

kitchen after a meal. *"You wash. I'll dry."* Sleeves were rolled up and hands were plunged into deep, porcelain sinks filled with warm, sudsy water.

These were the days when clanging kettles pulled from cupboards could be heard daily in every kitchen, instead of the now-familiar beep of a microwave unthawing a frozen dinner packaged by a stranger in a factory a thousand miles away. Truly, is there anyone among us who isn't delighted to hear the clatter of pots and pans in the kitchen knowing that a home-cooked meal is about to be prepared?

Ingredients originated in your backyard and were also purchased from the grocery store downtown, owned by a local family, not a chain store. Purchases were bagged in paper sacks, then carried out to your car and loaded for you. They called it service. Elderly folks in frail health could telephone in their weekly list of needed items and expect a bag boy to deliver their order. Grocery stores made house calls, and so did doctors.

If you happened to stop for a few gallons of gas on your way home, a friendly attendant would pump your gas, check your oil, and wash your windshield—all for free! *Who doesn't miss this—especially when it's raining!?*

Merchants had their own doorway—the baker, the florist, the butcher, and the man over at the hardware store. These were businesses owned by generational families who had served their community in the same capacity for years. We remember the names and faces of these men and women who stood behind the counter and waited on us. Strip-malls didn't exist, nor did one-stop-shopping megastructures. Stores were closed on Sundays so families could spend time with one another. *(It was the law!)*

Cathy Stern

Outside of town, farmers were active in fields, and wives kept busy in the kitchen, making the most of every morsel—especially during the Great Depression years of the 1930s when both food and money were scarce. Nothing could be wasted—particularly food—because it was not uncommon to have a dozen mouths to feed in a single family. It was a time in our nation's history when people went to bed hungry and woke up the same way—a worry most of the younger generation of today can say they have never had. The depression lasted a full decade and is remembered as "the longest ten years in our nation's history."

The difficulty of providing nourishment for your family meant that carefully-tended gardens were "as big as the whole backyard" and hoes could be found in every garage. In addition, it was necessary for most families to search for anything they could find to supplement their food source—mushrooms, fish, wild game, and nuts (if you were smarter than the squirrel.) Red-ripe apples, gathered from orchards, were pressed into cider. Syrup was drawn from maple trees. Wild asparagus was located in a nearby ditch and carried home in one-gallon tin pails. So were blueberries.

Cooks had a genuine talent for making good use of everything. People lived by the belief that to "waste not" was to "want not." These were more than mere words; they were a way of living. If butchering a pig, it meant the entire animal would be put to good use "except the squeal."

Pork-roasts and beef-roasts were stretched into stew. Meaty bones were boiled into soup broth (much to the dismay of the family dog). Butter

The Salvation Army distributed food and gifts to needy families during the Great Depression. The crowd at this event in Indiana was standing room only.

was churned.  Pears and peaches were hand-picked and canned in tightly-sealed quart jars.  Cabbage was shredded and packed into stone crocks for sauerkraut. Raspberries and strawberries were turned into pint-sized jars of jelly.  Canned goods helped sustain families during the long winter months when the garden was buried beneath the snow. Long rows of neatly-stacked jars were lined up behind glass pantry doors, or were stored in a cool basement on makeshift wooden shelves.  Stone-walled cellars with dampened-earth floors helped preserve the autumn harvest for months—bushel-baskets of squash, gunny-sacks of potatoes, and carrots buried in sand.  Some vegetables and fruits even lasted until spring!

Many white-haired folks today, leaning on canes, still miss the gardens of yesterday, and the joy of having awakened to "the sight of things growing" when they were youngsters.  There was a certain thrill in picking an ear of corn in your backyard and eating it "five minutes after it left the garden," or screwing off the lid of a canning jar filled with pickles and dill sprigs, both pulled from the garden with your own hands.

Well-stocked cellar shelves were scaled back considerably when the great drought—"the dust bowl"—devastated the food supply of the entire Midwest in the 1930s.  Soil was turned to powder, and it blew away.  Crops withered and died.  So did the grass.  Years passed without a drop of rain—*yes, years*.  People pulled dandelions from the dry earth where grass had perished and ate the leaves as salad.

Mothers who had a genuine talent for making food stretch needed to be even more creative during the drought.  Housewives considered what could be made from everything. It took great skill for a woman to cook a meager pile of spuds into an oh-so-delicious kettle of scalloped potatoes, flavored with an old ham bone.

The Great Depression and subsequent drought years affected every aspect of a person's life—from food to clothing. Garments were worn until they were beyond mending. Socks with holes were darned, instead of thrown away. Patches were sewn on the knees of pants—and sometimes more than once. No one was embarrassed to wear hand-me-down clothes because you were in the majority, not the minority—especially outside the cities. If you were treated to a new dress, it was undoubtedly sewn by your mother from a flour sack. (Flour was sold in large, 50-pound fabric bags with printed patterns on them.)

Life continued to be economically difficult until the late 1940s because World War II followed the Great Depression and the dust bowl. Supplies were challenged again—food and

SWANS DOWN WARTIME RECIPES
CAKES · QUICK BREADS · DESSERTS

otherwise. The United States was engaged in the raging war from 1941 until 1945. Wartime cookbooks were distributed which promoted "point-stretching, money-saving" tips. These recipe books were an attempt to assist cooks in the kitchen during the lean years of the war when rations and narrow incomes reduced the supply of everyday goods we now take for granted. Sugar was rationed. So were butter, milk, and cheese. Shortening and lard were also limited supplies. Each family received ration stamps to purchase small quantities—very small quantities—of scarce items. Everyone "made do." "Sugar Shy" cookbooks instructed housewives how to make cookies and cakes with as little sugar as possible.

Coffee was another rationed commodity. Grounds were used and re-used, day after day, until the brewed pot was nearly as colorless as water. Complainers were reminded: "Someday you'll be weak and old, too."

Prosperity returned in the 1950s, and food was again in abundance, but if you were to ask almost anyone who grew up as a youngster during the 1930s and 1940s, they would be quick to tell you that their mothers and fathers did an incredible job of shielding them from the raw truth of those difficult days. Most would assure you that they never tasted cooking so delicious as they did in those bygone years when everything was made from scratch, a period when families had more time than money. This proved, in many ways, to be a treasure beyond measure. As one old-timer said about the years following the stock market crash of 1929: "When the banks closed, we opened our hearts."

Those long ago days of cookbooks and aproned mothers truly yielded more than lump-free gravy and over-sized kettles of soup—soups made with vegetables, dumplings, and beans, simmered to perfection on gas-lit stovetops. The real bounty of these memorable meals was the fellowship shared by those who congregated around the kitchen table for a sit-down supper, together, enjoying both the food and the company of one another, eating as a family and talking about nothing in particular—a father inquiring about a daughter's homework, a mother sharing news from a

---

## The Great Depression

From 1929 to 1933 the unemployment rate rose from around 3 percent to a staggering 25 percent, which translated to more than 13 million people unable to find work. (And those numbers didn't account for the millions more who were forced to take pay cuts and reduced hours.) Home foreclosures skyrocketed. Over 10,000 banks collapsed. After taking office in 1933, the worst year of the crisis, President Roosevelt tried every trick in the book to jump-start the economy, but nothing seemed to work. In 1939, more than a decade after the crash, unemployment was still in excess of 17 percent.

**MICHAEL WILLIAN**

---

letter received in the mail from a distant relative, a teenager warning a little brother to quit crossing his eyes or they would stay that way.

There was, and still is, a certain satisfaction in plain-spoken talk, in hearing someone ask you when you return home in the evening, "How was your day?" The time spent eating a simple meal with one another became a source of unity. Kitchens were places of sharing, and of caring, when the supper hour came.

Even though eating together was a nightly event, there remained something special about gathering together on Christmas around a table that could seat twelve (or more) comfortably. Maybe it was the cloth napkins or the extra-fancy silverware, used only for holidays. Or it could have been the carefully-placed porcelain china, handed down through the generations, laid exactly in its place on a freshly-starched linen tablecloth, ironed wrinkle-free. Perhaps it was the infrequent use of "the good dishes."

These fine details probably made their contributions to the merry scene, but the real magic of the moment came from the reunion of familiar faces gathered around a steaming turkey, baked to golden-brown perfection, or around a honey-cured ham, or a goose as big as a kindergartner.

Never have the words "the more the merrier" been more true than in the years of multi-leafed wooden tables that could be pulled apart and lengthened by several feet when company joined the meal. *Those were the days!*

Kinfolk arrived by the carload—everyone piling out. *What a sight!* Front doors opened, and hearty greetings were called: "Come on in out of the cold!" Loved ones, with arms fully extended, flung wide their welcome.

Overcoats were hung up (or placed in a large pile in the center of the bed), and everyone pulled one another close against their heart for a hug. Aunts and uncles pinched little cheeks, remarking at how tall the young children had grown since the last time they visited.

Then it was time to be seated on mismatched chairs for the feast. Every year, family, and extended family, came together in honor of Christmas, sitting closely around a table laden with holiday favorites, and in those moments, the memories of all that occurred around that table came rushing back, and it felt as if none of them had ever left.

Platters and bowls were passed from individual to individual, and drumsticks were vied over—so was the wish bone by the children after the meal. Aunts and uncles and all manner of cousins filled the tall, straight-backed wooden chairs. Happy faces spoke to one another across the dinner table, everyone talking at once—those with wrinkles and those with flesh as soft as a just-picked peach. The youthful "whipper-snappers" talked about their futures, and the elderly talked about their pasts, re-telling the old stories again. The middle-aged would smile and listen to the older folks, pretending it was the first time they heard the details of a story they had long ago memorized, with an ending they knew by heart, because they realized that those repeated stories would soon be missing. They understood that time passes, and so do lives, and the day would come, soon enough, when they would give just about anything to hear those familiar voices ramble on in their heartwarming way.

More than blood unites us. Our shared memories do, too. It is why we honor the important occasions with celebrations to gather the scattered family. It's quite a feeling to be surrounded by people who knew you from the first hour of your life. Their faces represent the history of who we are. They are a linked chain that unites our generations.

This feeling of togetherness was the thread that stitched the pieces of holiday tradition into a unison that became the whole of the season—tasty accompaniments and all.

And how grand it was when our noses recognized the scent of something familiar, a once-a-year kind of smell—a pie baked by a favorite aunt, or the exact proportion of sweet smelling spices a grandmother used in a signature dish—perhaps the stuffing inside the turkey—a recipe no one could ever quite duplicate because of her unique measurements, a "pinch" of this and a "dash" of that. Each bite could suddenly remind us that we were home, and it was Christmas, and there was no better place in the whole wide world to be at that moment than where we were.

These were the days when a woman knew how to thicken gravy, and how to punch bread dough down with her fist after the yeast made it rise. These were the days of red-checkered tablecloths, cast-iron frying pans, loaf pans, and potato mashers with wooden handles.

And these were also the days when a cook knew how to expertly double—or triple—a batch of just about anything when the Christmas season arrived. The kitchen was a favorite spot year-round, but especially during the holidays. If you walked past a heated oven in December, you knew—for sure—that something tasty was inside. (Although you didn't need to be in the kitchen to know it was Christmas; the aromas permeating the air were enough to tease your nose and assure you that the grand holiday approached.)

One of the most notable images that comes to mind when the idea of the holiday season is mentioned is the vivid picture of a wide array of home-cooked foods and sweets decorating tablecloths and countertops, complete in detail down to the smallest drip of frosting. Mouths can begin to moisten at even the thought of a baking sheet, lined with little balls of dough placed in neat rows, waiting for their turn on the oven rack. Mmmmm! These were not quick-and-easy, pre-packaged cookies from a supermarket shelf. No, these cookies were mixed from recipes handed down through generations. Christmas cookie baking meant the varied flavors of peppermint, cinnamon, nutmeg, and ginger—and vanilla, purchased from the friendly Watkins Man—added to a batch of buttery dough.

The best part of baking a platter full of treats wasn't necessarily eating the finished product. It sometimes meant treating yourself to a spoonful (or two, or three…) of the scrumptious, sugary dough as it was balled up. There was something special about taste-testing the "presults" of an old-fashioned recipe.

Other cookies were created by the motion of a heavy wooden rolling pin, flattening and smoothing a thick blanket of hand-kneaded dough on a countertop covered in flour. Then came the fun part—choosing a shape! Kitchen drawers rattled with the familiar clinking sound of narrow strips of tin bent into Christmasy shapes. These cutters were then pressed into service. Can you remember a favorite cutter your mother used every holiday? Was it a candy cane? A bell? Santa's boot? Bethlehem's star?

Christmas meant gingerbread men and gingerbread houses. It also meant fruitcake, peanut brittle, and fudge. And popcorn balls wrapped in red cellophane. And cookies flavored with chunks of chocolate.

Thinking back, it is almost possible to imagine the taste of one of those warm, milk-dipped cookies eaten slowly, each bite savored just a little more

# Christmas Cookies

than the last bite. A cup of cold milk was, and still is, the perfect companion for a warm cookie. (The milk in those days was, however, poured from a glass bottle delivered by the milkman to your front door—unless you lived on a farm. Then it was delivered straight from the barn.)

Christmas also meant sugar cookies latticed with colored icing, frosted one-by-one after the pan of baked goods had been transferred from

the oven to the cooling rack by a mitt-covered hand. Young girls were eager to assist with the time-consuming task of decorating—or any other kitchen activity. They studied the careful eyes and practiced hands of older women, slowly committing to memory the art of being a good cook. Lists of ingredients were reviewed, and recipes read. Years of know-how were required to develop the necessary skills to be considered "an expert" in the kitchen. Young ladies were encouraged by matriarchs who reminded them, "All it takes is practice."

Years would pass, and the truth of those words would come to be understood. Then, these grown-up little girls would repeat the same words to their children and grandchildren as they mixed a batch of Christmas cookies together.

While the bakery was later decorated, stories would be told about long ago days when people milked cows by hand and gathered eggs from a hen house, stories about fruit cellars and cisterns, smokehouses and outhouses, and "Sunday dinners"—baked chicken, country ham, pork chops and barbequed ribs—meals followed by contented sighs. Memories would be consulted concerning those distant days when hard work—and lots of love—went into the planning of meals.

Then it would be time for everyone to take their place and gather around the Christmas table once again.

Cathy Stern

# Deck the Halls

"The stockings were hung by the chimney with care, in hopes that Saint Nicholas soon would be there."

CLEMENT C. MOORE
*A Visit from Saint Nicholas*

 # *Deck the Halls*

Nothing quite says "deck the halls" like the sight of a trail of evergreen needles leading up to the front door, or smelling the scent of pine, the first fragrance of Christmas. Or hearing the creak of the attic stairs, youngsters knowing that Dad would be climbing upward in search of the holiday decorations, and the whole family would be helping to garnish every open space—indoors and out—with all manner of Christmas décor. The children, especially, were more than eager to lend a hand and, needless to say, with little ones assisting, not an ounce of angel hair or silvery tinsel was spared.

Celebrating Christmas in the large, two-story homes of the 1930s, 1940s, and 1950s was truly something special. It was an era of houses built to last—houses with high ceilings, wall-papered walls, hardwood floors, and lots of bedrooms, filled with lots of children.

The festive transformation of these homes during the Christmas season began with the turning of the calendar page from November to December.

**Robert May, creator of Rudolph the Red-Nosed Reindeer, decorated his family's home with an image of the icon.**

*Did you know . . .*

Rudolph the Red-Nosed Reindeer was originally named "Rollo" by his creator, Robert May, who was an advertising executive for Montgomery Wards. The name was then temporarily changed to "Reginald" before executives at the firm decided on Rudolph.

2.5 million copies of Robert May's story about Rudolph were given away free to shoppers at Montgomery Wards in 1939. The story was not re-printed again until 1946 when World War II ended. (There was a paper shortage during the war years. The shortage affected Christmas cards and wrapping paper, also.)

Robert May's brother-in-law, songwriter Johnny Marks, set the poem to music in 1947. Gene Autry, "the singing cowboy," recorded the song—the bestselling record of his career. The song was later recorded by Bing Crosby, Perry Como, Lawrence Welk, and Guy Lombardo.

Male and female reindeer both have antlers. However, male reindeer shed their antlers before the Christmas season begins, while female reindeer retain their antlers throughout the season.

There was a special feeling that arose at hearing the creak of those stairs and seeing the dusty boxes pulled from secluded corners, then lowered down. Usually, the unmarked boxes had been stored hurriedly the

season before allowing a small surge of wonder to accompany the lifting of each corrugated cardboard flap, as forgotten collections of holiday tidbits were revealed. This afforded a small ceremony at the outset of the season which brought the same anticipation as opening a gift.

Each room was given thought and care as decorations—rotund-bellied Santas and snowmen crafted from styrofoam balls—were distributed throughout the house. Miniature figures of Mary and Joseph, and wisemen and shepherds, ceramic with chipped paint, were each unwrapped from their tissue paper storage and assembled beneath the roof of a wooden manger. The entire ensemble, complete with camels and oxen and sheep, encircled the infant Jesus who had been gently laid on a bed of real straw.

Wooden banisters of open staircases became spirals of pine as they were draped in garlands of real evergreen and topped off with red bows.

Fastened to fireplace mantles were stockings, homemade and sewn in red and green. Many of these were lovingly made by a mother or grandmother, talented homemakers well-experienced in the art of sewing, and boasted the name of each child in large embroidered letters across the cuff, stitched by hand, to ensure that Santa would not deliver your goodies to a sibling's stocking. The era brought several lean years, as well—times when Christmas stockings held little more than a few peanuts and an orange tucked into the toe.

Decorating an entire house was not a quick process, especially those tasks of untangling long strings of Christmas lights, and hanging thin strips of tinsel on the tree, one strand at a time, the placement of each chosen carefully. Strings of brightly-colored lights needed to be checked and double-checked, bulb by bulb, to ensure proper illumination. A single faulty bulb could darken the whole string. This time-consuming task often required a second mug of hot chocolate—or even a third—before the challenge of locating non-lit bulbs was complete.

Even the kitchen held a touch of festive décor with holiday tins waiting to be filled with edible contents, the once-a-year kind of yuletide bakery that told you it was Christmas—fruitcake, gingerbread men, and sugar cookies decorated with colored sprinkles and hand-mixed frosting. Advent calendars, filled with twenty-five pieces of chocolate, each molded into a unique holiday shape, were hung from kitchen walls, making children wild with Christmas anticipation. Each tiny door was opened, day by day, to reveal a treat hidden behind it. It was a yummy countdown to Christmas!

Above doorways hung fresh greenery and sprigs of mistletoe, awaiting holiday kisses below. The season's Christmas cards, and even some of the favorites from holidays before, were pinned around door frames, adding archways of cheer.

And, of course, there was the ceremonial placing of ornaments on the tree. Christmas trees, usually erected in generously-sized corners, or positioned centrally in front of a large window at the front of the house, told of the bringing together of ornaments collected through the years. These tokens came from many places and many years, their histories held dear to the families who trimmed the branches with sparkling splendor each and every season.

FIREPROOF
SPUN GLASS

Oz.

# Angel Hair

The most cherished ornaments were often not the ones with the highest price tag, or even those sold in stores at all. They were, as they still are, those ornaments created by children, carried carefully home to proud parents in schoolbags. What a feeling to return to your childhood home as an adult, years later, and recognize ornaments dangling from tree branches that were crafted in your childhood.

Whether decorating a home or a classroom, it just wasn't Christmas until crooked rings of paper chains, strips of red and green construction paper fastened with thick globs of paste, or homemade "glue" made from flour and water, hung from the upper corners of doorways and from the flexing branches of Christmas trees. Paper chains were often partnered with long lines of cranberries patterned between bits of popcorn, hand-strung.

Few areas within a home were left untouched by festive decorations. Small Christmas trinkets could even be found swinging from white-porcelain doorknobs, positioned just above skeleton-key peepholes. Beyond the decorated knobs of front doors awaited a new playground ready to be decked with its own array of festivity—the outdoors.

The outsides of houses were colored with the green leaves of holly and the red of berries and bows. Lights were strung from rooftops and porch pillars, and from shrubbery and trees, their large glass bulbs casting a soft glow in reds, greens, blues, oranges, and yellows, reflecting upward from the white, snowy ground. Boughs of woven evergreen branches were fastened to picket fences, and wreaths were hung from front doors—and

sometimes from an outhouse door, as well. (Many rural homes in the 1930s and 1940s did not have electricity or running water.)

Families strolled, especially at night, down snowy streets lined with mature trees—oaks, maples, and elms—past their neighbors' homes, folks they knew on a first name basis. Everyone was out—bundled from head to toe in hats and gloves and scarves, with only eyes and noses exposed—to gaze at an array of decorated scenes that gave each lawn its own holiday uniqueness. The festively-decorated streets added a local charm that united even strangers driving through with the common bond of Christmas spirit.

Winter itself was probably the grandest decoration of all, transforming the landscape into a whitened scene, making the world look like the front of a Christmas card. And even if the snow hadn't fallen yet, you could still dream of a white Christmas as children crafted intricately-cut snowflakes to hang from soon-to-be frosted windows. All that was needed to simulate a flurry of flakes were a few sheets of white paper, each folded in half, and in half again, and a sharp scissors.

Classrooms were maybe the most uniquely decorated places at Christmastime, holding the magical touch of unbound childlike creativity. Chalkboards became palettes for pictures of reindeer and elves. Santa cutouts with cotton-ball beards hung from desks. A mosaic of artwork lined the walls and sparkled with the unmistakable shimmer of excessive glitter. The little ornament-makers remained hard at work in 4-H clubs and at troop gatherings with the Boy Scouts and Girl Scouts of America. Truly, it

was the handiwork of youngsters that made Christmas special for parents, as it still does today.

Communities, too, readied themselves for the grand holiday. Decorations were hung from lampposts lining the drives of towns and cities. Lights were strung across Main Streets and across bustling downtown city centers, brightening sidewalks along entire city blocks, creating an experience that could not be found elsewhere.

City squares held famously large Christmas trees, wrapped round and round with strings of colorful lights, illuminated at spectacular tree-lighting ceremonies. Crowds, numbering in the thousands, gathered on snowy sidewalks surrounding city trees to take part in the yuletide fun.

Entering a department store was like stepping into another world—glistening decor surrounded shoppers as they came and went. Nothing was decked out more elaborately than department store windows at Christmas.

For the youngsters, stores transformed toy departments into "Toylands," "Joylands," and "Maybe Lands"—beautiful winter wonderlands, ensembles of spectacular decorations with moving, mechanical characters that simulated what it might be like to visit the North Pole and enter the workshop of Santa Claus himself. At no other time of the year did it seem more possible for dreams to come true for a child than at Christmas.

How could a child not believe in the magic of the Christmas season, when each year decorations and symbols retold the stories of reindeer that could fly and Santa's big bag that could hold enough toys for all boys and girls everywhere?

*Let there be light!*

**Throwing the power switch to illuminate downtown Chicago, 1947**

DoNTOpen FC

Until
Christmas

Cathy Stern

# Season's Greetings

"The mailbox brightens the roadside, and the letters inside brighten my heart."

ELEANOR BILLINGS

# Season's Greetings

A postcard for a penny, a stamp for three cents.

Christmas cards from the 1930s, 1940s, and 1950s brought the enjoyment of hearing from family and friends you hadn't heard from since the season prior.  It was a period of time when hand-written letters were part of the culture and the principle means of communication. Families wrote letters because they could seldom afford a long-distance telephone call.  These calls were expensive—and simply not in the budget.  This wasn't necessarily a bad thing.  It only meant that you were that much more excited to tear open an envelope addressed to the entire family—especially at Christmas.

Greetings shared "tidings."  They were a way to connect with loved ones during Christmases past when travel was limited.  They were also a way to send a "holiday hello" to a friend or neighbor who lived next door—or down the street.  There was, and still is, something special about conveying the sentiment "I remember you" for only the price of a sheet of paper and a single stamp.

"You've got mail" meant physically walking to your mailbox—whether indoors at the post office or outside at the end of your drive—to retrieve your post where the mailman delivered it.   Bundles and bundles

**Christmas mail
December 23, 1931**

of brightly-colored envelopes were sorted by postal workers as Christmas neared. Lines lengthened. December was a month when an abundance of cards and letters arrived, but not credit card bills because credit cards did not exist. People made purchases only if they had the money to pay for them. *Imagine that!*

Holiday editions of magazines like *The Saturday Evening Post, Harpers Weekly,* and *Life* were also delivered to postal boxes. People looked forward to their arrival during the season.

Families living apart from one another exchanged lengthy "Christmas letters," annual summaries of events that occurred during the preceding year—ordinary and otherwise. Readers learned who lost a tooth and who brought home a stray kitty named Pork Chop. They learned who could sing the A,B,Cs and who enrolled in college. Births were announced, and so were weddings—with newsy details and "wish you were here" notations. It was always a thrill, also, to find a photo enclosed with the letter and see the smiling familiar faces you had missed over the months—or sometimes years. *My, how the children had grown!* These letters were signed by loved ones with a distinctive handwriting your heart could recognize and sealed

## Price of a Postage Stamp

| | |
|------|---------|
| 1930 | 2 cents |
| 1940 | 3 cents |
| 1950 | 3 cents |
| 1960 | 4 cents |

**Vintage Christmas card**

inside envelopes postmarked with stamps that needed to be licked in order to stick.

There were fewer distractions in the olden days, so correspondence was read and re-read. Folks truly cared about the events that happened in another person's life and savored every heartfelt word someone had taken the time to share.

Letters from long-distance relatives were often accompanied by packages postmarked from faraway places. There was a real excitement when you spotted the postman coming up the walk with an armful of boxes, each wrapped in brown paper and secured with a length of string. Children watched excitedly from windows, even though they knew they wouldn't be allowed to unwrap the string-tied parcels until Christmas Day. In the meantime, however, they were eager to give each package a good shake, taking a guess at what might be hidden inside! If a box was addressed to Mom, the contents could be a fruitcake, or maybe a batch of homemade cookies. It wasn't so much what was inside those packages that mattered, however; it was more about the fact that someone had thought of you.

Mail was cherished between 1930 and 1960, but never more treasured than it was during World War II. The United States Postal Service set a record for the most mail circulated in 1941 following America's entrance into the war. A ceaseless flow of outgoing and incoming post followed as able-bodied men were ferried across the Atlantic and Pacific Oceans to serve abroad. Homesick soldiers half a world away eagerly awaited any word from home, and the postman became "the most important man of the day."

Military personnel hastened to answer letters, using their lap as a desk, and mailing their responses back in envelopes that didn't require stamps—only the word "free" written in the upper right-hand corner.

With a heavy load of mail traveling back and forth from military bases to the United States during the conflict, a new method was needed to

save on transport space, and V-Mail was created. (The "V" was a symbol popularized during the conflict years, standing for "victory" to inspire depressed spirits during long absences from anything that resembled home.) V-Mail involved a system of photographing a message written on a one-sided form, and printing the image on a much smaller 5" x 4" sheet of photographic paper, which greatly reduced the space necessary to ship large quantities of correspondence.

Admiral William Halsey protested visits from Washington diplomats to the frontlines during World War II because the additional weight of each person on the airplane made it necessary for precious mail to be removed from transport cargo space to compensate for the human cargo. He was quoted as saying: "Please stop the flow of Washington experts and sightseers. Each expert means two hundred less pounds of mail. I'll trade an expert for two hundred pounds of mail anytime." Admiral Halsey understood that these letters from home meant the world to weary soldiers serving in distant places and brought, at least for a moment, ear-to-ear smiles. Morale was boosted during "Mail Call" when there was little left to boost. Letters brought soldiers a feeling of being closer to loved ones back home, lessening their loneliness. A lump would rise in a soldier's throat as he sat in his barrack, slowly reading correspondence which told him in silent description the life his family was living in his absence. Newborn babies, who fathers had not yet had the chance to see, were quickly growing into toddlers as the months, and years, passed without return.

Many times, a wife or mother had no contact with a husband or son—

other than an exchange of handwritten letters, and perhaps an extremely rare long-distance telephone call—for years at a time. Soldiers' efforts were fueled by hope, and that hope came from the vicarious interaction with family.  Husbands kissed wives with X's and O's, and fathers attended children's Christmas pageants through written words and snapshots enclosed in letters.  This communication, however brief and seemingly impersonal, was a great comfort.

Soldiers left loved ones behind who promised to "write every day," and they did.  Their letters, addressed to names and serial numbers, included sentiments like "come home safely" and "I miss you."

With the war's end, life returned to a happier time and the mail carrier's bag was again filled with cards and correspondence sent from familiar locations.  As Christmas neared, children sharpened their pencils and wrote the all-important letters of the season—letters that began with the words "Dear Santa."  Youngsters worked tirelessly writing to St. Nick, assuring him that they had, in fact, been extra good that year.  If they *hadn't* been on their best behavior, an explanation for any potential naughtiness was jotted down, the fault of which was usually attributed to an older sibling.  These letters, addressed to "Mr. and Mrs. Claus" at the North Pole, were piled high in mailrooms across the country.

There were other fun aspects to Christmas postal traditions, as well.  Many families mailed their cards and letters to post offices located in festively-named destinations such as Santa Claus, Indiana, where the correspondence was stamped with a special holiday logo—adding

Christmas cheer to the face of the envelope.

Christmas cards.  They were as important to holiday celebrations in years gone by as baking goodies and hanging ornaments.  Letter carriers, with their mailbag strap slung over their shoulder, were a welcomed sight as they carried the annual well-wishes of families throughout the neighborhood.

# Festive Postmarks

## North Pole, Alaska 99705

It's Christmas every day in North Pole, Alaska! Here, visitors can have their photo taken with real reindeer—Prancer, Comet and Cupid (all in year-round residence when they are not helping Santa deliver gifts).

North Pole's post office receives hundreds of thousands of letters addressed to Santa each year, and thousands more from people wanting the town's postmark on their holiday greeting cards.

Visitors to North Pole are able to purchase a letter *from* Santa, as well, at the Santa Claus House in town. (The letters are available in many languages.)

## Santa Claus, Indiana 47579

Yes, Virginia, there is a Santa Claus! And it's in Indiana! This community is situated around three lakes: Lake Holly, Christmas Lake, and Lake Noel. Street names in Santa Claus include Mistletoe Drive, Jingle Bell Lane, and Arctic Circle.

The world's largest selection of gourmet candy canes can be found at the Candy Castle, and shopping baskets at Holiday Foods grocery store are red and green.

Everyone is a believer in Santa Claus, Indiana!

## Bethlehem, Pennsylvania 18015

The city of Bethlehem was founded on Christmas Eve, 1741. It is nicknamed "Christmas City, USA" because of its annual holiday festivities. America's first Christmas tree was erected in Bethlehem.

A large star shines brightly over Bethlehem every night of the year, from 4:30 p.m. until midnight. The star—*which can be seen from twenty miles away!*—was erected on top of South Mountain in Bethlehem. It measures 81-feet high by 53-feet wide. Signs surrounding the community read: "Follow the Star to Bethlehem."

# Joy to the World

"For unto you is born this day in the city of David, a Savior who is Christ the Lord."

GOSPEL OF LUKE

# Joy to the World

*"I heard the bells on Christmas Day, their old familiar carols play, and round and sweet the words repeat of peace on earth, goodwill toward men."*

Christmas just wouldn't have been Christmas for most families in decades past without hearing the sound of heavy brass church bells ringing, summoning worshippers in welcome to a Christmas morning service or a Christmas Eve candlelight gathering.

Christmas meant hearing a pipe organ playing familiar carols—*Away in the Manger, Hark the Herald Angels Sing, O Little Town of Bethlehem*—the same songs you had heard since as long as you could remember.  It meant feeling the weight of a heavy hymnal in your hand, and singing along in unison, following printed lyrics across a thin page.  And it also meant listening to special choir anthems, duets, and solos—*O Holy Night* or *Ave Maria*—the crescendo of uplifted voices creating a reverent awe in the sanctuary.

Today, the heart of Christmas can sometimes get lost in a bustle of activity, but in the past, church life marked the cornerstone of a community—especially in smaller rural towns where one could often see the peaks of multiple steeples rising high above neighborhood homes. It was a period of time when "shining up" for church was as important as

**Scrub-a-dub in a tub**

showing up—at Christmas and otherwise. After all, "cleanliness was next to Godliness."

Scrubbing yourself clean in the 1930s, 1940s, and 1950s often meant accomplishing it in a large tin washtub filled with sudsy water on Saturday night. A single washtub had to, many times, suffice for bathing an entire family because long, hot, lavish showers did not exist—especially for rural families when indoor plumbing was not yet available to them.

Youngsters were urged to wash behind their ears and scrub between their toes. Shoes were polished, and teeth were brushed with baking soda. Dresses were ironed, and fathers drew sons' neckties snuggly around the collars of freshly-starched white shirts tucked neatly into trousers. Mothers set hair in curlers, and tied ribbons around their daughters' pony-tails and pig-tails—or positioned barrettes.

Once everyone was looking their "Sunday best," families headed to worship in their shiny shoes, with parents shuffling children along to the same steeple-topped sanctuary where generations of their loved ones had,

more than likely, been baptized, confirmed, and married—all under the same roof. Tradition was cherished, and well-kept.

Once inside the church, you were greeted with the firm handshake of an usher positioned just inside the large front doors—probably a man you knew all your life. Bulletins were offered with a smile as the inflowing congregation proceeded down the center aisle between long rows of thick, wooden pews. Men, women, and children sat shoulder to shoulder, crowding in—quickly filling the church to standing-room-only capacity during holiday services. Mothers held infants on their laps—babies wearing cloth diapers and rubber pants.

No matter how many times you had attended a service, it was irresistible to take a momentary gaze upward at the high, vaulted ceiling, or at the ornate stained-glass windows visually telling Biblical stories. Heavy brass chains suspended light fixtures above those seated below, illuminating the congregation, as well as the altar's focal point where children would soon deliver a pageant worthy of adoring awes.

One thing that was sure to be anticipated at a church service on Christmas was the singing of long-ago memorized carols—*Joy to the World, The First Noel, God Rest Ye Merry Gentlemen.* Generations of your family might sing along with you, everyone happily inclined to sing just a little bit louder than at most other regularly-held services.

It was often a tradition in many churches to offer at Christmas, instead of a typical sermon, a children's pageant to deliver the nativity story to all in attendance. This involved children rehearsing their lines for

weeks in advance, youngsters practicing their memorization in front of brothers and sisters in the family living room at home after supper, with mothers urging from the background, "slower" and "louder."

And who could forget the joy of watching excited youngsters, from toddlers to teenagers, costumed in bedsheets secured with safety pins, performing the Christmas story, bloopers included?  The building echoed with the drumming of little footsteps marching in dis-union down the center aisle.  Then, one by one, tiny shepherds, angels, and wise men, along with Mary, Joseph, and baby Jesus—someone's doll from home—took their places "on stage" and began the show, right on cue. *Almost!*

The wide stairs at the front of the chapel became the rolling hills outside Bethlehem, and a small crowd of baby-faced shepherds, their dimpled smiles shining brighter than Bethlehem's star, were greeted by a whole sky full of angels, each heavenly host flapping his or her tiny wings, constructed from carefully-twisted wire hangers and stretched cheesecloth. Childlike improvisations gave an authenticity that couldn't be duplicated. "Fear not, for I bring you tidal waves of great joy!"  A child's tiny voice was greeted by the adoring smiles of parents, brimming with pride.

Once the long-cherished Christmas story was delivered, the service concluded with the singing of *Silent Night*. All was calm, all was bright. Hand-held candles were lit for the song, and soft shadows rose and fell with the flicker of the flames. "It was never Christmas," remembered one elderly grandmother, "until I was sitting in church on Christmas Eve singing *Silent Night*."

## Pageant rehearsal

There came a hush of quiet as the carol ended and the closing prayer was said. Heads bowed and hands folded. It felt good to have heard the old story, told and re-told across twenty centuries, a story of kings kneeling in adoration and shepherds beholding a star.

Worshippers were comforted by the tradition of gathering together in a church pew to sing and pray while being drawn nearer to the heart of that which was truly Christmas.

# Billie-the-Brownie

"You remember radio, don't you?  Radio provided the sounds, and you provided the picture.  Radio gave you thumps and crashes, laughter and screams, and you pasted them together with your imagination."

**WILLIAM JANZ**

# Billie-the-Brownie

We all know the magical story of Santa's wonderland workshop by heart, a place teeming with busy, pointy-toed elves laboring day and night building toys for the world's children. In this frozen Christmas kingdom, hidden due North, you will also find Santa's favorite elf, Billie-the-Brownie.

Billie was a character dreamed up by advertising executives in the late 1920s at Schuster's Department Store in Milwaukee, Wisconsin, for a promotional campaign. (The store later merged with Gimbels.) The little elf burst into fame so quickly that by 1931 he had his own radio program, airing daily at 5:00 p.m. between Thanksgiving and Christmas. For over twenty-five years, Billie became as much loved as Santa Claus to children growing up in the Midwest during this time. Every Christmas, for nearly three decades, Billie brought stories of the North Pole to life—first in print ads and parades, then in voice. Wide-eyed children wearing Billie buttons waited breathlessly, plopped down on their tummies in front of radios watching the clock tick, anxious to hear the program's opening music, *Jingle Bells,* and the toot of a tin horn announcing they would soon be greeted by voices coming all the way from the top of the world—*"Hello, boys and girls!"*

What a thrill! Tots were regularly informed by Billie on how things were progressing at the workshop.

This was a period of time before television, and entertainment was largely reliant on personal imagination. There were no bright colors and animations flashing across a wide screen, only the crackling of voices protruding through a thin layer of static, supported by primitive, yet successful, sound effects.

The mind of a child truly has the power to create wonders given even the smallest nudge, and radio allowed its listeners to fashion characters merely through thought. Yes, Billie lived at the North Pole, but more importantly, he lived inside your imagination. He was so real to boys and girls; they could almost see him coming out of the radio.

Billie entertained waiting ears with up-to-the-minute reports concerning Santa Claus and his far-removed world—from prancing reindeer to Mrs. Claus baking cookies. On one episode, Jack Frost came by the workshop to borrow paint brushes from the elves after they finished using them. "Oh, if Jack wants to borrow the brushes so he can paint windows with frost," said Santa Claus, "let him have them. He always brings them back again in the spring."

Kids sat side-by-side, staring at the lit dial on their radio, mesmerized. "Calling the North Pole, calling the North Pole," came Billie's voice through artificial static which was meant to sound like a short-wave radio Billie used when he was away from the North Pole checking on children.

During each broadcast, the beloved elf reached into Santa's mail bag and pulled out several letters. Then he read them aloud over the airwaves, making sure to include each child's name and address. Youngsters were raised to celebrity status by their peers if their wish list was chosen by Billie! Because of this, mail poured into the radio station, and continued to pour in, for a quarter of a century—*hundreds of thousands of letters would arrive in a single season!* Listeners were kept in suspense until the next day's episode by the hope of Billie reading their letter. Programs concluded daily with Billie reminding kids: "Tune in tomorrow to hear your old friend."

Billie's show captivated children and, at the same time, pleased parents with its moral lessons. The program stressed good behavior under the guise of "Santa and Billie are watching you." As a result, children helped wash dishes and offered to set the table. Homework was done on time, and even the rowdiest of youngsters could be found using proper table manners. Listeners were urged to "brush teeth, eat vegetables, and be kind to siblings."

This feat of obedience was accomplished with the help of Billie's magic book—a storybook, locked and sealed, containing holiday tales. During each episode, Billie asked boys and girls if they had been good that day, and they would answer out loud, declaring in unison: "I have been good!" (This was the "key" to opening the magic book.) The book, much like Santa, had the power to know if you were telling the truth. The pages would unlock only if children had indeed behaved, and Billie would then go on to read a short Christmas story. Every now and then, however, the

book would fail to open. Then, each child was left wondering if maybe it was something that he or she had done which caused the pages to remain shut—like not picking up toys or acting naughty at school. *Oh, the relief when the magic book squeaked open—and the disappointment when it didn't!* This tactic enthralled little ones who were drawn to the show, and also impressed parents by improving the behavior of their rascals.

Programs ended each year with the all-important, and long-awaited, Christmas Eve broadcast from the frosted realm as Billie helped Santa prepare for his lengthy trip around the world. Reindeer were harnessed, and the toy bag was hoisted into the sleigh. Santa reminded Mrs. Claus to hang up her stocking by the fireplace, and she promised to have his pipe and slippers waiting for him in the morning when he returned home.

Tots sat captivated in front of their radio, turning up the volume knob, hardly able to believe Santa's sleigh was preparing for takeoff—and they were right there listening to everything!

Raymond McBride, a former little kid—and Billie fan—remembered these holiday broadcasts from his childhood:

"The big moment always came, of course, on Christmas Eve. Santa created suspense with technicalities that threatened to delay his departure from the North Pole, while children at home groaned anxiously. Eventually though, Mrs. Claus admonished her husband with, 'Hurry, Santa! If you don't get going, you won't make it around the world tonight!' Then Santa climbed into his sleigh, and 'to his team gave a whistle,' and off the reindeer went, with all the appropriate sound effects: runners creaking through the

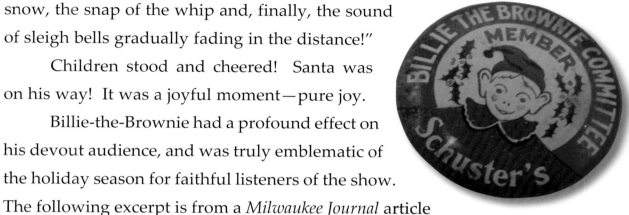

snow, the snap of the whip and, finally, the sound of sleigh bells gradually fading in the distance!"

Children stood and cheered! Santa was on his way! It was a joyful moment—pure joy.

Billie-the-Brownie had a profound effect on his devout audience, and was truly emblematic of the holiday season for faithful listeners of the show. The following excerpt is from a *Milwaukee Journal* article containing a letter written to the Editor by a mother of an avid Billie fan. The letter, signed "Just Old Memories," was a touching tribute to what the character meant to her child.

*Just after Pearl Harbor, my son left for service on December 17, 1941. In April 1942 he was shipped out to an island in the Pacific. He was in all the rough stuff such as the invasion of Tarawa. Of all the Marines who went in, only about 1,500 came out in one piece, alive. We did not hear from him for many months, and we did not see him for three years, from 1941 until he got his first furlough and was home for Christmas again in 1944.*

*My son was helping me trim the Christmas tree on Christmas Eve. It was just before supper, so he listened to Billie-the-Brownie on the radio. (Can anyone remember how touching it was when Santa told everybody goodbye before he left the North Pole?) Our son sat on the floor by the radio, and he began to cry so hard. I asked him, "What is the matter?" He told me, "Mother, I am crying because I am so happy. I cannot explain it in words, but I am home after where I have been, and after what I have been through. I am back here, sitting and listening to Billie-*

*the-Brownie once more."*

During the war years (1941-1945), radio broadcasts were filled with updates on the fighting. You could barely escape the thought of it. However, Billie-the-Brownie's show was different. The show's creator and producer, Larry Teich, promised to keep Billie's broadcast "a daily oasis, free of any thought of war," filled only with yuletide cheer. "All through World War II," said Teich, "Billie never mentioned the war once. We thought of it as a 15-minute sanctuary, sacred to children. Parents wrote in to us saying how much they appreciated this."

Billie's program remained a long-time favorite, but like most good things, it had to reach an end somewhere. The popularity of television had attracted a significant portion of radio's audience by the 1950s and, because of this, it was suggested that Billie-the-Brownie be converted to a television program. Larry Teich, however, protested. "You cannot put a picture on a screen as pretty as a child can dream," he said.

The memories of Billie—and the emotions the show instilled—live on, as real today as they were in Christmases past. The mere mention of Billie's name to white-haired members of the older generation is enough to vanish the years from their eyes and leave them wondering, "Has all that time really passed?"

# Acknowledgments

Works by Norman Rockwell are printed by permission of the Norman Rockwell Family Agency, copyright 2008, Norman Rockwell Family Entities; "It's a Wonderful Life" image: *Copyright Melange Pictures LLC, all rights reserved, courtesy of Paramount Pictures*; Brach's Candy image: *Permission granted by Farley's & Sathers Candy Company, Inc.*; Howdy Doody image: *Courtesy of Memory Lane Syndication, a division of MediaNet Group Technologies. www.doodyville.com 1-954-974-5818;* Macy's parade photo of "The World's Largest Stocking": *Courtesy of Goodyear Tire & Rubber Company and University of Akron Archival Services Department, Akron, Ohio*; Macy's advertisement ("We've enlisted!"): *Used with permission of Macy's Corporation, New York, New York*; "Scared of Santa" photo (child on Santa's lap): *Courtesy of the Maryjane Mendrick private collection*; Lionel Train images: *Courtesy of Lionel LLC, New York, New York*; Peter Pan record: *Courtesy of Inspired Studios, Livingston, New Jersey (formerly known as Synthetic Plastics, Newark, New Jersey)*; Girl with doll/sled photo (pg. 41) and two girls with a toboggan photo (pg. 15): *Courtesy of the Linda Vis private collection*; NOMA Christmas Lights images: *Courtesy of Inliten, LLC, Glenview, Illinois*; Angel Hair and Tinsel Rain images: *Used by permission of Santa's Best*; "Christmas Cookies" recipe book cover: *Image used courtesy of the Wisconsin Electric Power Company collection*; "How to Bake by the Ration Book" image: *Courtesy of Kraft Foods, Inc.*; "Sugar-Shy Baking and Cooking" recipe book: *Image courtesy of Integrys Energy Group*; Pennington family photos (pg. 161 and 162); Three letter carriers photo (Image DN-0009469): *Used by permission of the Chicago History Museum*; Mail carrier delivering Christmas mail (Image DN-0090217): *Used by permission of the Chicago History Museum*; Mail carrier delivering Christmas mail (Image DN-0090218): *Used by permission of the Chicago History Museum*; "White Christmas" image: *Copyright Paramount Pictures Corporation, all rights reserved, courtesy of Paramount Pictures*; 1936 gas prices photo with Walter Linge: *Courtesy of the Walter and Esther Linge private collection*; Ice skating photo, parade photo (with Santa/reindeer), and "Hi, Santa!" photo: *Courtesy of the Milwaukee County Historical Society*; The Old Farmer's Almanac image: *Reprinted with permission of The Old Farmer's Almanac, Dublin, NH. Learn more at Almanac.com*; Robert May hanging Christmas lights with two daughters and Rudolph photo: *Copyright 2008 by Robert L. May Company LLC, used by permission of the Robert L. May Company*; Christmas furlough photo and family of four caroling photo: *Courtesy of the Claire Whitney private collection*; Walgreen's diner photo: *Used with permission of Walgreens Corporate Communications, Deerfield, Illinois*; Santa Claus image on back cover: *Used with permission of Ideals Publications LLC, a Guideposts company, Nashville, Tennessee*; Photos courtesy of the Sheboygan Falls Historical Research Center: *Sorting Christmas mail, husband and wife cutting a Christmas tree, two children rolling snowballs, child in a snow tunnel, adults building a giant snowman, downtown street decorated with American flags, and 1936 automobile driving on snowy roads*; Barnum's Animal Crackers image: *Courtesy of Kraft Foods, Inc.*; Photos courtesy of the Chicago Public Library, Special Collections and Preservation Division, include: *Christmas Shoppers, 1936 (Image CLAC 1-30-6), Christmas Shoppers, 1936 (Image CLAC 1-30-7), Christmas Choir, 1941 (Image CLAC 2-2-12), Children looking at window, 1943 (Image CLAC 2-11-2), Christmas promotions—throwing the power switch to illuminate downtown Chicago (Image CLAC 3-11-1), Santa Claus, 1947 (Image CLAC 3-11-11), State Street decorated with candy canes on light poles, 1949 (Image CLAC 3-15-8), Children with large candy cane, 1949 (Image CLAC 3-15-39)*; Children with letters to Santa photo (pg. 155) and pageant rehearsal photo (pg. 165): *Used by permission of Getty Images*; Photos courtesy of J.C. Allen & Son, Inc.: *Cover photo (boy at window), book jacket photo (woman decorating snowman), two boys with sled throwing snowballs (pg. 4), boy gathering wood (pg. 11), boy on pedal-tractor (pg. 35), men with bicycles (pg. 73), mother canning (pg. 109), Great Depression gathering (pg. 113), mother baking cookies (pg. 122), and family in window (pg. 135).*

*An Old-Fashioned Christmas* features the watercolor paintings of Cathy Stern. The authors extend deepest gratitude to the artist for her generosity of spirit and commitment to the project.

If you would like to learn more about Cathy Stern's wonderful artwork, including original paintings, Christmas cards, and reproductions, please contact:

Cathy Stern
W4967 River Road, Fredonia, Wisconsin  53021
1-262-305-6686

*"Working with watercolor is truly an exciting and responsive medium. I also enjoy working with pen, pastels, and pencils.  Patience is mandatory, as well as an open mind and free spirit."*

CATHY STERN

The authors extend appreciation to the Milwaukee County Historical Society for use of the Billie-the-Brownie images included in *An Old-Fashioned Christmas*.  Gratitude is further extended to WTMJ Radio for permission to include broadcast material from the Billie-the-Brownie radio program.

The CD included with this book contains a sample of an original Billie-the-Brownie broadcast archived by the Milwaukee County Historical Society. To purchase additional programs on CD, as well as Billie-the-Brownie memorabilia, please contact the Milwaukee County Historical Society at 1-414-273-8288. Your purchase directly supports their education and preservation programs.